BIRTH CONTROL

Birth Control

ALAN E. NOURSE, M.D.

Franklin Watts
New York/London/Toronto/Sydney/1988

Illustrations courtesy of Anne Canevari Green

Library of Congress Cataloging-in-Publication Data

Nourse, Alan Edward.
Birth control.

Includes index.
Summary: Explains the process of reproduction and
why and how birth control is used. Describes
different methods of birth control, their rates of
effectiveness and their drawbacks.
1. Birth control—Juvenile literature. [1. Birth
control] I. Title.
HQ766.8.N68   1988   613.9′4   87-21604
ISBN 0-531-10516-4

CONTENTS

Chapter One
The Whats and Whys of Birth Control
11

Chapter Two
How Pregnancy Happens
19

Chapter Three
How Birth Control?
39

Chapter Four
"Natural" Methods of Birth Control
49

Chapter Five
Barrier Methods of Birth Control
67

Chapter Six
The Pill
83

Chapter Seven
Other Hormone Contraceptives
99

Chapter Eight
Intrauterine Devices (IUDs)
111

Chapter Nine
Sterilization
119

Chapter Ten
Abortion
135

Chapter Eleven
Birth Control in the Future
143

Glossary 149

Index 155

BIRTH CONTROL

1

THE WHATS AND WHYS OF BIRTH CONTROL

This book is about birth control—what it is, how it works, and why the plain facts about birth control can be so vitally important for all young people to know.

Probably every girl at one time or another has her own private dream of someday becoming pregnant, having a baby, and raising her own family under ideal circumstances. And although they might not admit it, most teenage boys, at one time or another, have very similar dreams of someday becoming fathers, having their own sons or daughters, homes and families. Nothing could be more natural than for young people to have such dreams—without them the world would be a pretty dismal place.

It's also natural that young people, as they pass through **puberty** (the time of life when they begin to mature both physically and emotionally), will begin to explore the sexual part of their lives that will eventually make those dreams possible—not only the natural sexual feelings developing in their own bodies, but the whole world of sexual relationships with others as well. This is one of the greatest and most exciting explorations of a person's lifetime. The development of loving relationships, the establishment of new families, the natural fulfillment of having children—in fact the survival of the whole human race—depend on it.

Often this great exploration may seem like a carefree and adventurous game. But that game has certain rules dictated by nature. Of all the people in the world, approximately half are physically equipped sometime to become pregnant and to carry and deliver babies. The other half must contribute in their own way in order to make those pregnancies possible. Pregnancies occur according to very specific rules and, from puberty on, most people are driven by their sexual natures toward a natural goal of reproduction. This is true of all living creatures—but in our human society pregnancy and childbearing are not 100 percent desirable at all times and under all circumstances. In fact, there are times and circumstances when a pregnancy can be very undesirable indeed.

FOUR PEOPLE, FOUR PROBLEMS

For Jennifer L. it was wedding bells at the age of nineteen. She and her fiancé had a beautiful summer church wedding two weeks after Tom's graduation from the state university, and the young couple have a bright future planned. Tom, at age twenty-two, has a good job with a decent starting salary and good career prospects. Jenny has two more years of nurse's training to go and then wants to practice nursing for a while before starting a family. Tom, whom she met two years before, has always been "Mr. Right" for her and shares her desire to have children someday, maybe two or three, when the time is right—but not right away. Not until she's finished her training, at least, and has some career experience behind her. . . .

A pregnancy right away is not part of their plans. Of course, Jenny knows that it wouldn't be a total disaster—

but if she has to drop out of nurse's training to take care of a new baby, it might be very hard to go back later, and she doesn't want that to happen. And that means that she and her new husband need to find a way to keep Jenny from getting pregnant, if possible, until the right time arrives. It's as simple as that.

For Donna M., age fourteen, "Mr. Right" has come along a few years too early, and there isn't any wedding in the plans. She thinks she's in love with Eddie, but whenever they're together he wants her to have sex with him, and it's more than she can do to put him off. Now she's constantly worried about getting pregnant. All she knows about "birth control" is using a vinegar douche after sex, and she knows of other girls for whom that hasn't worked too well. There isn't any help at home—her father hasn't been around for years, and it's one big fight after another with her mom. It's hardly any wonder she feels trapped and scared.

The way things are going, if Donna isn't already pregnant, she soon will be. For her there is no way that being pregnant can be anything but bad news—in our society a pregnancy in a fourteen-year-old girl is practically *never* desirable. What Donna needs desperately is some competent advice about how to keep from getting pregnant until some time in the future when having a baby makes some kind of sense.

Dixie P. has a totally different kind of problem. At age thirty-eight, she is a happily married housewife with three healthy children, the youngest already twelve years old. Dixie has been using "the Pill" for birth control off and on for years, dropping off just when she and her husband chose in order to space their children two or three years apart. Now, however, things have changed. First, her doctor thinks she should now stop taking the Pill for health reasons, because she's older than thirty-five. But at this point in her life, she feels that a new pregnancy would be a real disaster —she doesn't want any more children, *ever*. Dixie doesn't want just any old substitute for the Pill—she wants a substitute that's 100 percent sure. Fortunately, she and her husband have several good choices available. Their problem is deciding which one will be the best for them.

For Beth T., age twenty-seven, other circumstances apply. Beth is the busy owner of an interior decorating studio. She thinks of herself as a dedicated career woman. She's never married and doesn't plan to, although she has a close and loving relationship with John, with whom she has been living for more than four years. Beth doesn't think she *ever* wants children, and neither does John—but she knows she might change her mind someday, so she doesn't want to do anything permanent to damage her ability to become pregnant later. As for birth control *now*, she wants something both extremely reliable and essentially hassle-free. She doesn't want to take pills, or take special precautions for sex ahead of time, or fiddle around a lot afterward. With all these specifications, Beth's choices are fairly limited, but she still has a few. She just has to decide which one, for her, will be the least trouble.

These four women are as different from each other as anyone could imagine, but they all have two major things in common. First, they are all *sexually active* in ways that would make pregnancy very likely if nothing were done to prevent it. Second, they all want very much to avoid pregnancy, although for totally different reasons. All four of them need some safe, effective, and reliable method of birth control.

WHAT IS BIRTH CONTROL?

By the very broadest possible definition, "birth control" refers to *any means a person can use to prevent or postpone getting pregnant and having a baby, or to avoid causing a pregnancy to occur,* more or less at the will or direction of the individual person. People often think of this as applying to the woman alone, but of course it applies to the man as well. The term **birth control** covers the ground from begining to end. At one extreme, a person who abstains from any sexual contact whatever is practicing birth control in its most effective possible form, as long as this abstinence, or **celibacy,** is maintained. People who take religious vows of celibacy, for example, use this form of birth control. At the other extreme, a woman who has a **hysterectomy** (surgical removal of the uterus) for any one of many reasons will have complete, permanent, and irreversible birth control as a result.

In between these two extremes, there are many different ways that birth control can be accomplished. Some methods are based upon preventing **conception**—preventing the male sperm and the female egg cell, or **ovum,** from getting together so that fertilization can take place. This type of birth control is called **contraception** (that is, "against conception") and devices or medications that make this possible are called **contraceptives.** Other methods of birth control seek to prevent an already fertilized ovum from becoming implanted in the woman's uterus in order to grow into a pregnancy. Although technically the terms **birth control** and **contraception** mean slightly different things, often they are used interchangeably to mean "measures to prevent pregnancy," as in this book.

Many people make a distinction between "natural" and "artificial" forms of birth control. So-called natural forms of birth control do not involve any kind of artificial intervention—no mechanical devices, no medicines, nor any other "outside the body" means of preventing pregnancies. The most commonly used natural method—withdrawal of the man's penis before ejaculation—is just not very effective, as we will see in chapter four. The other "natural" method is based upon a woman guessing as closely as possible when during her menstrual cycle she is most likely to become pregnant, and then avoiding intercourse at those particular times. This is often spoken of as "the rhythm method." To use it with any degree of success, a woman must have a very detailed knowledge of all the significant events in her own fertility cycle.

In contrast, artificial forms of birth control may employ mechanical or chemical barriers to conception, or hormone medicines to prevent ovulation, or other hormones to make it hard for a fertilized ovum to become implanted in the uterus. This distinction between natural and artificial methods is especially important for men and women with religious convictions that prohibit any artificial birth control methods but permit natural methods to be used.

There is certainly nothing new about the idea of birth control. Women and men have been looking for ways to prevent unwanted pregnancy since the beginning of history and have used all kinds of methods, some more successful than others. History tells us that women in ancient Egypt sometimes placed honey in the vagina before intercourse. (We know today that honey can effectively destroy both bacteria and sperm cells.) What is more, paintings on Egyptian tombs indicate that the men sometimes covered their penises with brightly colored linen, a sort of primitive form of contraceptive sheath. In the Middle Ages, penile sheaths made of oiled linen or sheep intestine were used, and the **condoms** available today may have acquired their name from a Dr. Condom who attended King Charles II in seventeenth century England and recommended such sheaths to protect the king from venereal diseases (infections transmitted by sex) and illegitimate children. According to eighteenth century records, half a lemon was sometimes inserted into a woman's vagina before intercourse both as a barrier to sperm and a sort of acid spermicide, and throughout history douching with salt water or diluted vinegar has been a commonplace approach to birth control. Unfortunately, many of these ancient methods were either extremely faulty or largely ineffective. It was not until perhaps 100 years ago that any really effective artificial birth control methods appeared, and even those were far from ideal.

THE IDEAL CONTRACEPTIVE

Suppose there were an absolutely ideal birth control method available—what would it be like? First of all, it would always work, 100 percent of the time, when the sexual partners didn't want a pregnancy to occur—but it would be quickly and completely reversible any time the partners decided they wanted to have a baby. It would be effective immediately whenever it was used—no waiting period— and would be permanently on guard until it was reversed, so that nobody would even have to think about pregnancy. And finally, it would have no undesirable side effects of any sort on either partner, nor interfere in any way with later childbearing ability at any time after it was reversed.

If there were such an ideal birth control method available, this would be a very short book, because nobody would be interested in anything else. Unfortunately, there's no such thing—not one of the birth control methods we will discuss in this book even approaches that ideal. *None* of them is 100 percent effective all the time under all circumstances. Most of them are neither instantly effective nor instantly reversible. And almost all of them involve *some* possible undesirable side effects, in some cases serious enough to be of real concern.

This means that any woman who wants to prevent or postpone pregnancy needs to know something about the whole range of birth control methods available. A method that might be just right for one woman could be all wrong for the next one, because different people have different needs at different times. And the same woman might need different kinds of birth control at different times in her life. Consider the four women we just talked about. All of them need a birth control method that will be as effective as possible. The young woman in nurse's training and recently married has several choices available—she merely wants to postpone pregnancy for a while. For the fourteen-year-old, a pregnancy would be a disaster; she needs a method she can really count on right now, one that will not damage her ability to have babies later on. For the older woman who already has all the children she ever wants, a permanent, irreversible birth control method such as sterilization may be the best possible choice—but not for the career woman who might someday change her mind about having a baby.

For any woman to pick a birth control method best suited to her particular needs and circumstances, she needs to know what different methods there are, how they work, and what particular advantage and disadvantage each may have to offer. All successful birth control methods depend upon one of two basic things: either preventing a male sperm from meeting and fertilizing a female ovum, or, if fertilization has already taken place, preventing the fertilized ovum from developing into a pregnancy. But to understand clearly how *any* form of birth control can work, we first need to understand the basic facts about both the male and female reproductive systems—about how the man's body produces sperm cells, how the woman's fertility cycle works to produce egg cells, and how and when, in simplest terms, a woman can become pregnant in the first place.

2

HOW PREGNANCY HAPPENS

There is only one way that a woman can become pregnant. A sperm cell from the male must meet and join a ripened egg cell, or **ovum,** from the female to form a new and very special kind of cell: a **fertilized ovum.** Two unusual biological events are necessary for this to happen. First of all, these special sex cells—the sperm cell from the male and the ovum from the female—must be formed in the first place. Second, these special cells, sometimes called **germ cells,** or **gametes,** must possess a special biological ability to join together, or fuse, into a single cell, the fertilized ovum, which then has the power, eventually, to develop into a completely new individual.

NORMAL CELLS
AND "HALF CELLS"

Most cells in the body do not have this power to fuse together. They exist separately, side by side, and each cell is biologically *complete*—that is, each cell contains all the genetic material necessary to create two complete new cells when it divides into two, as cells often do. This "genetic material" is actually coded information that determines every living thing's **heredity**—the passing of characteristics from parents to children. We know today that this genetic code is contained in molecules of a protein substance called **deoxyribonucleic acid,** or **DNA,** in the cell's interior nucleus. The DNA molecules there join together to form structures called chromosomes. (See figure 1.)

In human beings, each complete cell normally contains 46 chromosomes—23 neat little pairs. Each chromosome contains its DNA in little clusters called **genes,** which determine each person's individual physical characteristics —gender, hair and eye color, the size and shape of the body, etc. The body grows when these complete cells divide, a process called **mitosis.** When such a cell divides, each of its 46 chromosomes first splits down the middle, with half of each one going to either side, so that each of the two resulting "daughter cells" ends up with 46 chromosomes, just like the original "parent cell."

Things are interestingly different in the case of the special sex cells—the male sperm cells or the female ovum. These cells, when they are formed, are *not* complete cells with 46 chromosomes each, like other cells in the body— they are only "half cells" because they contain only *one* chromosome from each pair, or a total of 23 chromosomes each. This occurs because, when they are formed, their parent cells do not split each chromosome in each pair down the middle as happens in ordinary cells. Rather, the chromosomes in each pair simply pull apart, with *just one* of each pair going to each "daughter cell." This form of cell division, confined to only the special sex cells, is called **meiosis** to distinguish it from ordinary mitosis.

THE SPECIAL CELLS OF LIFE

Because these special sex cells, or gametes, are only "half cells," they cannot divide again to produce new cells as can

CHROMOSOMES

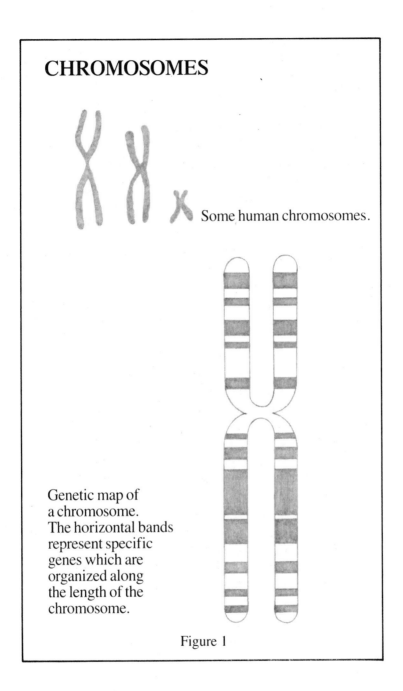

Some human chromosomes.

Genetic map of
a chromosome.
The horizontal bands
represent specific
genes which are
organized along
the length of the
chromosome.

Figure 1

ordinary cells. Compared to other cells, they live only a short while after being formed and then disintegrate. It is only when male sperm cells come in contact with a female ovum that these "half cells" are able to fulfill their special destiny. When this happens, the male sperm cells (usually present in large numbers) cluster around the female ovum on all sides until *one single sperm cell* succeeds in penetrating the cell wall of the ovum and gets inside.

Once this has happened, a remarkable biological event takes place. The 23 chromosomes from the penetrating sperm cell immediately line up with the 23 chromosomes in the nucleus of the ovum to form the 23 new chromosome pairs—46 chromosomes in all—of a normal, complete cell. But these chromosomes have not all come from one parent cell. *The sperm cell and the ovum, each from a different parent, have each provided half.* Doctors would say that the ovum has been fertilized. This fertilized ovum now has the potential to divide and redivide until, eventually, if it finds a safe place to grow and be nurtured, it will develop into a completely new and different human being—a baby with characteristics inherited from both the mother and the father, but an individual totally different from either one.

Obviously these male and female sex cells are very special, and they are manufactured in special places and special ways in the male and female bodies. To understand how they are formed, and then brought together to cause a pregnancy in the woman, we need to know something about the sexual organs and sexual functions of both men and women: the male and female **reproductive systems.** And since the male system is by far the simpler and easier to understand, that is the place to start.

THE MALE
REPRODUCTIVE SYSTEM

When a baby boy is born, he is already equipped with the male sexual organs that will enable him to become a "sperm producer" and a father when he finally reaches sexual maturity, sometime between the ages of eleven and fourteen. Most of the male **genitals,** or sex organs, are located externally, outside the body. The **penis** is a tubular organ located between the boy's legs. Behind the penis is a sac-like pouch of skin, the **scrotum,** which contains two oval sex glands known as **testicles,** or **testes.** These glands are composed almost entirely of miles and miles of tiny tubules lined on the inside with special cells known as interstitial cells. Above the testicles on each side these tubules empty into a larger conducting tube knows as the **vas deferens.** These tubes extend up into the pelvis (the lowest part of the abdomen) on each side and empty into small storage sacs called **seminal vesicles** that lie alongside the **prostate gland.** The seminal vesicles, in turn, empty into the **urethra** —a tube extending all the way from the urinary bladder above, down through the whole length of the penis to the outside. The male urinates through this tube and also discharges sperm cells through it, although always at different times. We see this male sexual apparatus diagramed in figure 2.

During childhood these male sexual organs are underdeveloped and inactive; the only hint we have of their eventual function is that, even in tiny babies, blood vessels in the penis sometimes become engorged and cause the penis to enlarge and stiffen temporarily in an **erection.** But around the age of eleven or twelve (sometimes a little earlier, sometimes later) a group of chemicals known as **hormones** begin to trigger some striking changes in the body's reproductive system.

Hormones are powerful chemicals produced in various parts of the body which travel in the bloodstream and stimulate biochemical changes in distant cells or organs. They are sometimes called "chemical messengers." At about the age of eleven the boy's testicles begin producing special male sex hormones called **androgens** which bring about widespread changes in the boy's body. First they stimulate

THE MALE
REPRODUCTIVE SYSTEM

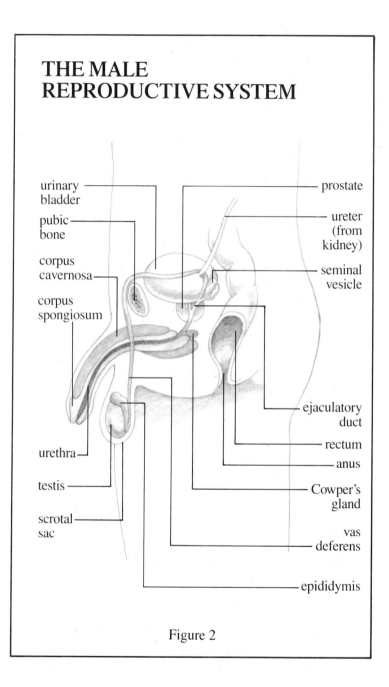

urinary bladder

pubic bone

corpus cavernosa

corpus spongiosum

prostate

ureter (from kidney)

seminal vesicle

ejaculatory duct

rectum

urethra

anus

testis

Cowper's gland

scrotal sac

vas deferens

epididymis

Figure 2

a burst of growth bodywide: the boy shoots up in height, his bones grow longer and stronger, and his muscles develop size and strength. He begins to develop pubic hair between his legs, as well as hair under the arms and, eventually, the first evidence of a beard. His voice box begins to enlarge, often quite suddenly, so that his voice begins to crack and then drops to a lower register. At the same time, and due to the same hormones, his penis, scrotum, and testicles begin to grow and mature; he becomes aware of increasing sexual feelings and interests, and tends to have more frequent erections. We speak of all these changes as **secondary sex characteristics**—indirect signs that his sexual organs are becoming prepared for their primary purpose of reproduction. The timing may vary from one person to another—it happens sooner to some and later to others, but sooner or later it happens.

At about the same time, other hormones appear, with a different kind of job to do. One of these, produced in the **pituitary gland** (a small organ connected to the underside of the brain) and released directly into the bloodstream, is known as **interstitial cell stimulating hormone,** or simply **ICSH.** When this hormone reaches the maturing interstitial cells in the testicles, it causes them to begin dividing rapidly. But under this hormone's influence, these cells don't produce more interstitial cells; instead, they begin producing large numbers of the special male sex cells, or sperm cells, we mentioned earlier. Those sperm cells pass up through the vas deferens and are stored in the seminal vesicles near the prostate gland.

THE LIFE OF
THE SPERM CELLS

The male sperm are produced in enormous numbers—hundreds of millions of them at a time. As we have seen, they are special "half cells" containing just half the normal number of chromosomes, one from each pair. They look different from other cells, too. Sperm cells are very small and oval shaped, separate and free from each other. Each one is equipped with a long, whiplike tail. Once released in a liquid medium, they swim around vigorously by lashing their tails, like so many tiny tadpoles.

Once the production of sperm cells begins in the male, it goes on continuously, day after day, year after year, until the extremes of old age. But where do all these sperm go? By the time they first appear, the young man is sexually mature and subject to both physical and emotional sexual stimulation. When sexually stimulated, his penis becomes enlarged and erect, sufficiently long to penetrate deeply into a woman's vagina. If the sexual stimulation continues, he will suddenly "come"—the sperm collected in his seminal vesicles, mixed with a fluid from the prostate gland, will suddenly be discharged, or **ejaculated,** through the erect penis during a male **sexual climax, or orgasm.** During sexual intercourse with a woman, this discharge of fluid and sperm, known as semen, is deposited deep inside the woman's vagina, right at the lower end of her uterus. During masturbation (self-stimulation without intercourse) it is simply lost to the outside. Sometimes semen may be discharged spontaneously while asleep during a sexually stimulating dream, a so-called **nocturnal emission,** or "wet dream." But the vast majority of the time, most of the sperm cells that are produced simply die in the male body and are reabsorbed, to be replaced by a virtually endless supply of new ones.

Outside the body the sperm tend to die very quickly—within an hour or two at the most. But if discharged into a woman's vagina during intercourse, vast numbers of them may survive for much longer—several hours at least, and sometimes even days—and they are very motile (swim around vigorously). At a time when a woman is fertile, they can make their way up through the lower opening in the uterus and on up into a Fallopian tube, still very much alive. And if the sperm meet up with a mature ovum in such a place, fertilization and subsequent pregnancy are very likely.

THE FEMALE
REPRODUCTIVE CYCLE

From the time of puberty on, the male will ordinarily produce sperm continuously for the rest of his life. This means that he is constantly fertile and capable of making a woman pregnant at virtually any time. Only under very unusual circumstances will he become infertile, or sterile. (A case of mumps during young adulthood, for example, may occasionally damage the testicles so that sperm can no longer be formed.) This "constant fertility" of the male is balanced by a completely different situation in the female. In fact, a woman will ordinarily be fertile for just a short time— about forty-eight hours—approximately every month. The question is *which* forty-eight hours—and why she is fertile for only forty-eight hours at a time.

Except for the external entry to the vagina, known as the **vulva,** a woman's reproductive organs are all internal, located in the pelvis—the lowest part of the abdomen. The **vagina** is essentially an elastic tube or canal a few inches long which extends from the vulva up to the lower end of the **uterus,** or womb. This organ, about the size and shape of a pear, has a narrow lower end known as the **cervix** and an upper part called the body. Although the uterus has thick muscular walls, it also has an internal cavity. A very narrow canal, ordinarily plugged with mucus, extends through the cervix from the vagina into the uterine cavity. At the top of the uterus the muscular walls give way to a pair of tubes about an eighth of an inch in diameter, one on either side, known as the **Fallopian tubes.** The hollow interiors of these tubes open directly into the uterine cavity at the lower end. At the upper ends these tubes spread out into fingerlike tentacles that are in close contact with two glandular organs, the female sex glands, or **ovaries,** one on either side. We can see these structures diagramed in figures 3 and 4.

Just as the male testicles produce the male sex cell, the sperm cell, the ovaries in the woman produce the female sex cell, the **ovum** (plural: **ova**). But unlike the male, who produces millions of sperm more or less continuously, a female ordinarily produces mature ova only one at a time. When a female child is born, her immature ovaries already contain the forerunner cells—the "buds," so to speak—of all the mature ova she could ever possibly produce—as many as half a million of them. Each of these "buds" is surrounded by a little nest of cells properly known as an immature **follicle,** from a Latin word meaning "pod," or "shell." The ripening of these follicles, one at a time, to form mature egg cells, or ova, is an intricate process which begins when a girl reaches the age of puberty, sometime between the ages of eleven and fourteen, and once again is triggered by the action of special hormones.

The earliest of these hormones to act are female sex hormones, produced in the ovaries and known as **estrogens,** meaning, literally, "estrus makers," a term that applies to periods of special sexual readiness, or "heat," common to dogs, cats, and other lower animals. (Human females have no such special intervals reserved for sexual activity, but the term seems to have stuck.) Like the androgens acting in the maturing male, estrogens cause a growth spurt in the female. They stimulate the growth of pubic and underarm hair, cause the girl's breasts to begin to enlarge, and trigger the development of a layer of fat on the shoulders and hips that will change the girl's "string bean" appearance to a more rounded and curvy shape—typical female secondary sex characteristics. At the same time, they cause the girl's sex organs—vagina, uterus, Fallopian tubes and ovaries—to become more mature. Interestingly enough, the male and female sex hormones—androgens and estrogens—are not

THE FEMALE
REPRODUCTIVE SYSTEM

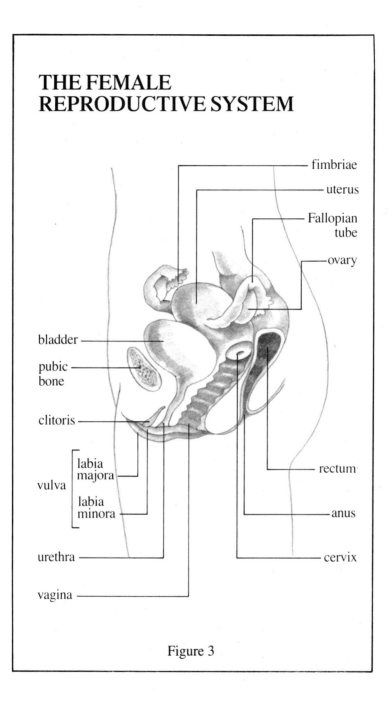

fimbriae

uterus

Fallopian tube

ovary

bladder

pubic bone

clitoris

vulva

labia majora

labia minora

urethra

vagina

rectum

anus

cervix

Figure 3

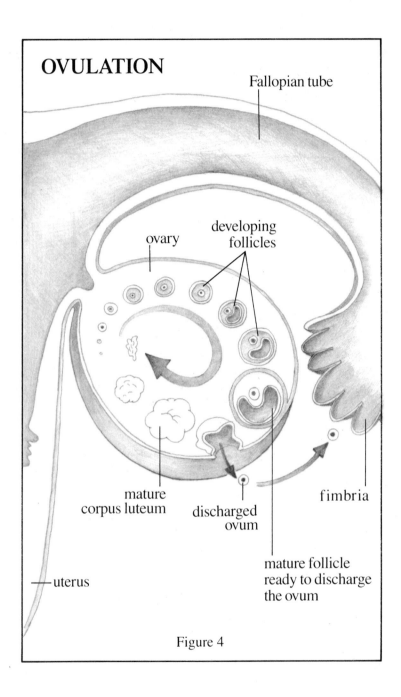

OVULATION

Fallopian tube

developing follicles

ovary

mature corpus luteum

discharged ovum

fimbria

mature follicle ready to discharge the ovum

uterus

Figure 4

possessed exclusively by males or females, respectively. Although the male has a preponderance of androgens, his body produces some estrogens, too, chiefly in his adrenal glands, while the female's adrenal glands produce small amounts of androgens. This accounts for the fact that girls suffer the hated adolescent plague of acne, or pimples, just as severely as boys do; the skin changes in acne are largely triggered by androgens. A girl doesn't have to have very much androgen to stimulate acne; a little bit is all it takes. But if she had no androgen at all in her body, she would not develop acne.

OVULATION:
NATURE'S GRAND ATTEMPT

Estrogens account for the secondary sex characteristics we mentioned above in the maturing girl and prepare her body for the first production of mature egg cells, or ova. But the actual production of those cells depends on the action of another group of hormones.

As we have seen, from birth on, a girl's ovaries contain many tiny, immature ova, just lying at rest in their nests, or follicles. For the first ten years or so of a girl's life, none of these follicles changes very much. Then, at around age eleven to thirteen or so, a special hormone is produced by the girl's pituitary gland, released in tiny quantities into her bloodstream, and carried to her ovaries. This hormone is called the **follicle-stimulating hormone,** or **FSH** for short.

As you might guess from the name, the job of FSH is to stimulate the growth of cells in the immature follicles so that the ova in their centers will begin to enlarge and mature. A number of follicles may be stimulated at the same time, and start maturing their ova, but usually one of the ova will begin to overtake the rest. This process will take about seven or eight days—and then a second hormone from the pituitary gland appears. This hormone targets the largest and most mature of the follicles, and triggers the final enlargement and ripening of the ovum inside, while the other ova stop growing Eventually the one fully mature ovum breaks free from the nurturing follicle and is caught in the upper end of the Fallopian tube that is wrapped around the ovary. Just as the male sperm cell is a "half cell" containing only half the normal number of chromosomes, one from each pair, the ripened ovum is also a "half cell" with just half the normal number of chromosomes.

Once the ripened ovum is free of the ovary and caught by the upper end of the Fallopian tube, it is slowly conducted down the tube, where it can come in contact with a sperm cell and become fertilized. This whole process—the enlargement, ripening, and release of an ovum into the Fallopian tube—is known as **ovulation.** You can think of it as nature's grand attempt to make reproduction possible. And simultaneously, other things are also going on to help this grand attempt succeed.

For one thing, as soon as the ovum is free from the follicle, that same "second hormone" that hurried the ovum-ripening process along earlier keeps right on acting on the follicle cells left behind in the ovary, causing them to form a small lump of pinkish-yellow tissue called the **corpus luteum** (from Latin words meaning "yellow body"). For that reason this "second hormone" is called **luteinizing hormone, or LH.**

At the same time, nature must provide the new ovum a safe place to grow and develop if it should happen to be fertilized by a sperm. Once again, it is hormones that set the stage. It takes about eight to ten days from the earliest ripening of an immature ovum to the time it is fully mature and released into the Fallopian tube. During that time, estrogens from the ovaries are very busy acting on cells lining the inside of the woman's uterus. The estrogens cause those cells to multiply very fast and to form special small blood vessels and tiny nurturing glands as they grow. By the time ovulation occurs, the uterine lining has become quite thick, with a rich blood supply. What is more, just after the mature ovum is released, that pinkish-yellow lump of tissue left behind in the ovary begins to produce a completely different hormone. Its job is to act on that enlarged lining of the uterus to make it soft and spongy and to make the glands begin to secrete sugars and other nutrients. This hormone has another job, too: it makes the thick mucus that normally plugs up the opening of the cervix turn soft and stringy, so that a sperm cell can have an easy time getting through into the uterus. This hormone is called **progesterone,** from Latin words meaning "ahead of pregnancy."

Finally, still another hormone, this one also from the pituitary gland, keeps prodding the corpus luteum to produce more and more progesterone, thus making sure that there is plenty of this "pregnancy-protecting" hormone around at the right time. Because this new hormone will later on work in partnership with estrogens to enlarge the woman's breasts and prepare them for milk production if she becomes pregnant, it is often called the **lactogenic,** or "milk-producing," **hormone,** or simply **prolactin,** which means "before the milk."

All this may seem terribly complicated at first glance, but actually it makes perfect sense once you understand the point of it. The woman's body is making a grand attempt at reproduction, producing a mature ovum ready to be fertilized and, at the same time, opening up an easy route for the sperm to follow and preparing a safe place in the uterus for the ovum to lodge and grow into a baby should it become fertilized. In order to accomplish all this, a whole series of events has taken place, each directed by a special hormone. But with one or two possible exceptions, there is no really good clue or signal to tell the woman that any of these hormone-directed activities is taking place. Once in a while, in some women, a bit of fluid may escape into the abdomen just when the ripened ovum breaks free from its follicle, and this fluid may cause some twinges of discomfort in the lower abdomen right at ovulation time. This discomfort, called **mittelschmerz** (a German word meaning "pain in the middle") can sometimes tell the woman that ovulation has just taken place. But since this happens to only some women, and then only sometimes, it isn't a very reliable sign of ovulation. An ordinary fever thermometer may provide a better signal: careful daily measurements of the body's temperature may reveal a slight temperature increase when ovulation takes place—a very useful clue, as we will see, for a woman who is eager to either become pregnant or to avoid pregnancy.

MENSTRUATION AND PREGNANCY

Obviously, up until ovulation, nothing is decided as far as nature's grand attempt at reproduction is concerned. It is only *after* ovulation that the all-important step can take place. At that time a particular ovum can meet up with a sperm cell and become fertilized. If this doesn't happen, the ovum doesn't last very long. If it isn't fertilized during sexual intercourse within about 48 hours, the ovum traveling down the tube into the uterus will simply disintegrate. The corpus luteum will then begin to shrink and stop producing progesterone. Several days later the specially prepared lining of the uterus, with its glands and many small blood vessels, will begin to break down. A quantity of discarded cellular material and a certain amount of blood will then pass down through the cervix into the vagina and be carried out of the body in a typical menstrual period. The amount of blood lost during menstruation is sharply limited because natural body processes soon pinch off the vessels supplying the uterine lining with blood. This allows the lining of the uterus to return very quickly to its original state, which it will maintain until the next ovum begins to develop.

Thus, menstruation is simply a temporary end point in

the female body's attempt at reproduction. The fact that a menstrual period occurs tells us that the attempt failed. The ovum was not fertilized by a sperm, so no pregnancy occurred.

Of course, the body doesn't stop after just one attempt. Soon after the menstrual period is over, the levels of follicle-stimulating hormone from the pituitary gland once again rise in the woman's bloodstream and trigger the ripening of another ovum. Estrogens again begin building up the inner lining of the uterus, the mature ovum is presently released into the Fallopian tube, and the whole **ovulation cycle** starts once more. If the woman never becomes pregnant, this cycle will be repeated over and over at roughly 28-day intervals (the exact time may vary widely from one woman to another) until she reaches her late forties or early fifties. At that point in her life a woman's production of sex hormones diminishes, she stops ovulating, and her menstrual periods come to an end—a time known as **menopause.**

Of course the story can be totally different if the woman has sexual intercourse several days prior to or during the 48-hour interval following ovulation, so that live sperm are present to meet the ovum. If fertilization takes place—and chances are about one out of four that it *will* if plenty of sperm are present in the right place (the Fallopian tube or uterus) at the right time—the fertilized ovum will then find its way down into the uterus and become embedded in the special lining of tissue that has been prepared there. Progesterone hormones will continue to protect and maintain the pregnancy and will soon stimulate the formation of a special organ known as the **placenta** to nourish the growing **embryo.** Soon the placenta itself will begin producing still more progesterone to help protect the pregnancy throughout its term.

Because this attempt at reproduction has succeeded, there will be no menstrual period. Instead, other hormone-induced signs of pregnancy will begin to appear—breast enlargement, for example, or episodes of morning nausea. What is more, the progesterone hormones also work to block the development of any new ova until the pregnancy is over, since the woman's body is normally only able to take care of one pregnancy at a time. The woman will not ordinarily begin ovulating again until at least two or three months after the baby is finally delivered, perhaps even longer. And the first evidence that she *is* ovulating again will be the appearance of the first normal menstrual period after her pregnancy is over.

Many women have the idea that since menstruation is so closely related to pregnancy, they can tell from their menstrual periods when they are likely to become pregnant. As we will see in chapter four, this just doesn't work. All the appearance of a menstrual period tells you is that a pregnancy probably has *not* occurred during the last ovulation cycle. If it had, there wouldn't be any menstrual period. But a normal period tells a woman nothing whatever about when her body will produce and release its *next* mature ovum. There is no set interval of time between the beginning of a menstrual period and the time of the next ovulation.

In fact, the only thing that *is* pretty reliable is the amount of time between ovulation and the beginning of the period that follows if fertilization doesn't take place. That interval is usually about 14 days and, within a day or two, applies to most women. Thus, when a woman's period begins, she can look back and say, "It must have been about 14 days ago that I ovulated." But there isn't any way to predict that critical ovulation time *in advance*, with any accuracy, from just the menstrual period alone.

Pregnancy, of course, is just the first step in nature's grand attempt at human reproduction. But, as we have seen, there can be many times and circumstances in which a woman may wish to avoid becoming pregnant, at least for the time being. Fortunately, there are a number of birth control measures that can be taken to help avoid unwanted pregnancies. With a basic understanding of how pregnancy happens in the first place, we can now consider some of the logical ways pregnancy can be prevented.

HOW
BIRTH CONTROL?

Considering what we know about how pregnancy happens in the first place, we can see a number of ways that pregnancy might possibly be avoided. Basically, a pregnancy depends on two "main events"—the fertilization of a ripened ovum by a sperm cell, and the implantation of the fertilized ovum in the uterus where it can grow. Almost anything one might do to prevent one or the other of those "main events" from happening could serve as an effective birth control method.

As an extreme example, have *no sexual contact at all*. If a woman were stranded alone on a desert island, she would not be in any danger of becoming pregnant—at least until she was rescued. Nor would a man stranded alone on a desert island run any risk of becoming a father. Of course, not many people are stranded alone on desert islands—but there actually are many people who practice short-term or long-term **celibacy** (no sexual contact at all) for a variety of reasons. Roman Catholic priests or nuns, for example, take religious vows of lifelong celibacy. Many families teach their young people that sexual contact should be post-

poned until after marriage, and husbands and wives sepa-
rated by circumstances often remain faithful, or celibate,
for long periods of time. Finally, concern about contracting
sexually transmitted infections such as genital herpes or
AIDS is making many young people think seriously about
celibacy until they are very sure which sexual partners they
want.

Such people aren't concerned with other birth control
methods; as long as they remain celibate, they know there
won't be any pregnancies. Similarly, people (whether male
or female) who are exclusively homosexual—male with
male or female with female—don't need to worry about
birth control, since pregnancy ordinarily requires male-
female sexual contact to happen at all. It is for people who
have male-female intercourse that birth control can be
vitally important.

"NATURAL" AND
BARRIER METHODS

Some such people prefer to avoid unwanted pregnancies by
so-called natural methods—that is, by *controlling* their
sexual contacts, or *timing* them in one way or another, so
that fertilization doesn't occur, but without using any mechanical devices or medicines to aid them in this goal. The
major "natural" method of birth control depends upon
identifying the woman's ovulation time with some accuracy,
and then avoiding sexual intercourse during the interval
before, during, and after expected ovulation, with sexual
activity resumed again only during the intervals when the
woman is infertile, or "safe." Since this means timing intercourse rather precisely according to the natural rhythm of
the woman's ovulation cycle, it is sometimes called "the
rhythm method" of birth control. For some couples this
method can work quite well; obviously, if intercourse is
scrupulously avoided whenever the woman has a ripened

ovum available for fertilization, and is not resumed until that ovum has disintegrated, pregnancy won't occur.

Unfortunately, this and other "natural" methods have serious pitfalls, as we will see in detail in chapter four. One way to avoid these pitfalls is to use some kind of a physical barrier, either mechanical or chemical, to prevent the sperm cells from reaching the ripened ovum. We will discuss a number of *barrier methods* of birth control, including the use of condoms and diaphragms, in chapter five.

PREVENTING OVULATION

The methods mentioned above depend, one way or another, upon preventing the sperm cells and ovum from coming in contact. A completely different approach to birth control, first widely used in the 1960s, involves the use of special hormone preparations to prevent ovulation from occurring at all. The rationale is obvious: if a woman doesn't produce a ripened ovum, as she normally would during her ovulation cycle, then there isn't any ovum to be fertilized, no matter when sexual contacts take place. The hormones necessary to prevent ovulation are taken regularly by mouth in the form of **oral contraceptive pills,** often spoken of collectively as **OC's,** or more simply as **"the Pill."** For many women the Pill is an ideal form of birth control, offering great advantages over any other method—but again, there are some pitfalls we will discuss in detail in chapter six.

PREVENTING IMPLANTATION
OF THE FERTILIZED OVUM

Even if ovulation has occurred and a ripened ovum has been fertilized by a sperm, it is still possible to prevent a pregnancy by preventing the fertilized ovum from becoming implanted in the uterus and growing. There are two main ways this can be accomplished. The first involves the use of special hormones to alter the lining of the uterus so that the fertilized ovum can't find a good place to become embedded. Without being embedded, it can't grow, and ultimately it disintegrates. In some cases, this kind of hormone manipulation can be used as a so-called morning after birth control method—sometimes used to prevent pregnancy "after the fact," in the case of rape, for instance.

A second approach to preventing implantation involves the use of a small plastic device inserted into the uterine cavity and left there for a period of time. This so-called **intrauterine contraceptive device,** or **IUD,** essentially acts as a foreign body in the uterus which causes the fertilized ovum to be expelled before it can get implanted. Although this birth control method is very effective, it can present a number of problems, which we will discuss in more detail in chapter eight.

PERMANENT BIRTH CONTROL

All the birth control methods we have mentioned so far are basically *reversible*—that is, they can be used as long as the woman desires to avoid pregnancy, but then can be discontinued to permit a pregnancy later, without having caused any permanent change or damage to the reproductive system. All these methods, however, have a basic flaw —although some work better than others, *none* of them works perfectly, 100 percent of the time, in all cases. **Sterilization,** on the other hand, is a comparatively permanent and totally effective form of pregnancy prevention— the ultimate "barrier method" of birth control. In the woman, it involves surgically tying off and severing the Fallopian tubes so that no sperm can ever reach a ripened ovum—a so-called **tubal ligation,** or **TL.** In the man, it involves cutting and tying off the vas deferens—an operation called a **vasectomy**—so that no sperm can ever reach the penis and thus can't be ejaculated during intercourse.

Sterilization in either the male or female has to be considered permanent. True enough, there are surgical techniques today which can sometimes—*sometimes*—restore the Fallopian tubes or the vas deferens to function later after they have been tied off. Unfortunately, these techniques often fail or, in some cases, can't even be attempted, and when they *are* attempted, the surgery is extremely difficult and costly, whether it succeeds or not. For this reason, most responsible doctors discourage sterilization except in the case of very mature individuals who fully recognize the probable permanent nature of the procedure and are virtually certain that they won't want either to have a pregnancy or to father a child under any circumstances in the future.

For women, another form of sterilization is *completely* irreversible: the performance of a **hysterectomy,** or surgical removal of the uterus. This is a major operation and is usually done for medical reasons that have nothing to do with birth control. Few doctors would recommend it *solely* for the purpose of birth control—but when a hysterectomy is performed, permanent birth control is one result.

ABORTION

For the woman who has become pregnant in spite of everything (or because nothing was done to prevent it) an **elective abortion**—the destruction and removal of an embryo from the uterus—is the only alternative to carrying the pregnancy and delivering the baby. Abortion is really a last resort in dealing with an unwanted pregnancy. It can hardly be considered a "birth control" method—in fact, in every sense it represents a flagrant *failure* of birth control. However, it is an important factor in many women's thinking about undesired pregnancy, and it is a fact of life, since a great many pregnancies are terminated in this way. Thus, in chapter ten we will present the facts about this procedure, how and when it can be safely done, and what problems may be involved.

A BIRTH CONTROL "MENU"

As we will see, some birth control methods offer special advantages to some women under some circumstances, while other methods may be better for others. To help avoid confusion, the following outline of methods—a sort of birth control "menu"—will help keep things straight:

(1) *Natural methods*—controlling or ordering intercourse in one way or another so that fertilization can't occur.

    (a) Celibacy
    (b) Exclusive homosexuality
    (c) *Coitus interruptus* (withdrawal before ejaculation)
    (d) The "rhythm method"—abstaining from intercourse except during "safe," or infertile, intervals. Requires identification of ovulation time with some accuracy.
    (e) Extended nursing

(2) *Barrier methods*—imposing a physical barrier (mechanical or chemical or both) between the sperm and ovum so that fertilization can't occur.

    (a) The condom or sheath
    (b) The diaphragm
    (c) The vaginal sponge
    (d) Spermicidal barriers (spermicidal vaginal foam, jelly, suppositories, vaginal film, etc.)

(3) *The Pill*

    (a) Basic Pill contraception—blocking ovulation

(b) Bi-phasic and tri-phasic pills

(4) *Other hormone methods*

    (a) The progesterone-only pill, or "mini-pill"—altering the cervical mucus to block the movement of sperm and altering the uterine lining to prevent implantation.

    (b) Morning-after contraception methods

    (c) Repository hormones for long-term effect

(5) *Intrauterine contraceptive devices (IUDs)*

(6) *Sterilization*

    (a) Vasectomy in the male (possibly reversible)

    (b) Tubal ligation in the female (possibly reversible)

    (c) Hysterectomy (irreversible)

(7) *Abortion*

(8) *On the horizon*—Refinements of existing methods; male birth control pills; and other new and/or experimental birth control methods still under investigation.

THE "GOLD STANDARD" OF BIRTH CONTROL

With all this variety of birth control methods, it's fair to ask: Why so many methods? Why not just one that all women and/or men could use? The answer is that no single method is absolutely ideal for everyone, or for anyone at all times.

    The first thing one wants to know in considering *any* birth control method is, simply, *how effective is it?* As we saw earlier, an absolutely ideal birth control method—the "gold standard," so to speak—would be 100 percent effective for any woman or man using it for as long as its use was continued. That would mean that there would be no unexpected pregnancy, *ever*, as long as the method was used. This "gold standard" for birth control just doesn't exist, for all practical purposes. As we will see later, even sterilization is not 100 percent reliable, because every now and then, for one reason or another, a sterilization procedure will fail. Only surgical removal of the woman's uterus can guarantee no unexpected pregnancy *ever*, and this is hardly a practical birth control method.

But if no method achieves the "gold standard," some come very close, while others don't. The Pill, for instance, may be more than 99 percent effective when properly used, while the use of a spermicidal vaginal foam alone may be only 80 percent effective. In other words, while the Pill is almost (but not quite) 100 percent reliable for preventing pregnancies, using spermicidal vaginal foam alone is nowhere near as reliable. But what exactly does "98 percent effective" or "80 percent effective" *mean*? Obviously nobody can become partly pregnant—you're either 100 percent pregnant or you're not, with nothing in between.

For any individual woman using any kind of birth control method, the method used will either protect her 100 percent at any given act of intercourse—she doesn't get pregnant—or it will protect her 0 percent—she does get pregnant. The percentage effectiveness of a birth control method is simply a measure of the *likelihood* that a woman will get pregnant over a given period of time using that method of birth control—that is, it is a measure of the likelihood that the method will succeed, or fail, compared to the "gold standard" of 100 percent effectiveness. In general, doctors use the term "percent effective" to refer to the number of pregnancies that will occur while the method is being used by a hundred women for a full year. If we say that the Pill is "99 percent effective," we mean that for every hundred women using the Pill exclusively for a full year, there will be only one unexpected pregnancy. Of course that one woman will be 100 percent pregnant. But if, for example, each of those 100 women had intercourse 100 times during the year, this would mean only one pregnancy per 10,000 acts of intercourse. By comparison, to say that spermicidal vaginal foam alone is only 80 percent effective means that for every 100 women using that method exclusively for a year, there will be 20 unexpected pregnancies, far too many to consider this a reliable form of birth control.

What can make a birth control method fail—or not fail? Any number of factors may be involved. In most cases failure occurs because the method isn't actually being used at all, or else isn't being used properly due to ignorance or misunderstanding. Obviously, a contraceptive diaphragm can't prevent a pregnancy if it's lying in the dresser drawer when intercourse occurs—but even if it *is* used, it may fail to prevent a pregnancy if a woman doesn't understand that it has to remain in place for six hours after intercourse to be effective, and thus unfortunately removes it too soon. Some birth control failures occur because of mechanical flaws—a condom that breaks during intercourse, for example. Hormone-type birth control methods may occasionally fail because a particular woman's body doesn't respond to the hormone as expected—but far more frequently because she forgets to take the Pill in the prescribed manner. Still other methods are just inherently imperfect: a chemical spermicidal barrier that only kills 80 percent of the sperm and allows 20 percent to get through unscathed is going to have a high failure rate. As we discuss each birth control method in turn, we will look not only at the relative effectiveness of the method, but also at any major points of failure, since knowing the weak spots in any birth control method is the first step to avoiding them.

ADVANTAGES, DISADVANTAGES, AND SIDE EFFECTS

Of course, reliability is not the only consideration in choosing a birth control method. How easy or difficult is the method to use? How much or how little does it interfere with such things as the pleasure, comfort, or spontaneity of sexual relations? A "natural" birth control method that leaves a woman constantly worried about whether it's going to work or not may be far more destructive to a normal healthy sex relationship than, say, a pill that is almost 100 percent reliable but may have some undesirable physical side effects. What about those worrisome side effects? And what other special considerations need to be taken into account? Some birth control methods, for example, require a doctor's examination, prescription, or guidance for use, while others can be used without professional consultation —as long as the person understands how to use the method effectively.

In almost every case we will find that a given birth control method offers special advantages balanced against certain disadvantages, certain considerations that may be favorable for one woman but, perhaps, unfavorable for another. As we discuss the various birth control methods noted in the outline above in detail in successive chapters, we will talk about the advantages, disadvantages, side effects, and special considerations of each method. The way to choose the best birth control method for *you* is first to understand all the ins and outs of each method, and then to decide what *you* think about sex and what will fit in best with your life, assuming that you don't want to become pregnant.

"NATURAL" METHODS OF BIRTH CONTROL

In seeking ways to avoid unwanted pregnancies, or in hopes of "spacing" children in some controlled manner rather than bowing to the whims of Nature, some people prefer "natural" birth control methods—methods that do not involve using physical or chemical barriers, or medicines (such as hormones) that interfere with the natural reproductive cycle. Many of these people are influenced by moral or religious codes that forbid any "artificial" tampering with the process of reproduction. Others simply don't want to take medicines or have mechanical devices such as condoms or diaphragms involved in their sex lives.

All "natural" methods depend, in one way or another, upon abstaining from intercourse during the intervals in the woman's ovulation cycle when she is most likely to have a ripened ovum available for fertilization, or else upon the use of sex techniques that avoid depositing sperm in the woman's vagina during her fertile periods. Of course such methods are not really "natural" at all, because they involve manipulating the timing or techniques of intercourse to achieve an "unnatural" goal: prevention of pregnancy. But they don't require any artificial, or "outside," mechanism to make them work. What is more, the widely used rhythm method can be at least fairly effective much of the time, and very effective indeed for some couples who use it faithfully and intelligently.

In primitive societies where no modern birth control methods were used, it was not uncommon for a woman to be pregnant regularly, every year or two, for twenty years or more. "Natural" birth control methods allow better control than that—but for many couples they are anything but reliable. Indeed, in overall practice, these methods are among the most unreliable of all the birth control methods available—but this relative ineffectiveness may not be so much the fault of the method as of the people using it. The overall ineffectiveness of "natural" birth control methods, as reflected in statistics, could be greatly improved if people using these methods understood more clearly how they were supposed to work and took greater pains to make them work properly.

COITUS INTERRUPTUS
(WITHDRAWAL
BEFORE EJACULATION)

In all history, this is probably the oldest of all birth control methods ever employed, and by far the least reliable for preventing unwanted pregnancies. **Coitus** (pronounced KO-ee-tus) is just a fancy medical term for sexual intercourse, and **coitus interruptus,** or "interrupted intercourse," is simply a matter of the male withdrawing his penis from the woman's vagina just before ejaculation so that his sperm is discharged outside the body. In theory, this technique ought to work to prevent conception even if intercourse occurs just after the woman has released a ripened ovum into her Fallopian tube and is at her very most fertile time—after all, if sperm don't reach that ripened ovum, fertilization can't take place. But in practice, the method fails almost as often as it works.

For one thing, this technique requires almost super-human effort and self-control on the part of the male. For a man, sexual excitement during intercourse occurs in an urgently rising crescendo terminating in an intensely pleasant climax at the moment of ejaculation. As that climax approaches, it is the man's natural instinct to thrust as deeply as he can—what better way for Nature to ensure that sperm are deposited just where they are needed the most for fertilization to be possible? It can be extremely difficult for a man to be sure exactly when his climax is approaching, and often almost impossible to withdraw in time to ejaculate outside, especially when this is exactly what Nature *doesn't* want him to do. Many men just can't do it at all; others may withdraw too late; and it may be impossible for the woman herself to pull away in time.

Even when withdrawal is practiced successfully, the method may still fail for another reason. As soon as sexual excitement begins in a man, there is a slight but continuing discharge of sticky fluid from the tip of the penis, and this discharge almost always contains sperm cells—not many, but some. It is perfectly possible for the sperm in this preliminary discharge to find their way up to a ripened ovum and fertilize it even if the main discharge of sperm during ejaculation doesn't occur in the vagina at all. (This, incidentally, accounts for the occasional woman who becomes unexpectedly pregnant after heavy petting, including contact of the penis with the vulva, but with no actual penetration of the vagina. The sperm cells have simply found their way to their goal from outside.)

For these reasons, withdrawal alone is probably one of the least reliable of all possible birth control methods and has been used less and less in recent years. Although failure rates are hard to establish, since people using this method aren't usually included in medical studies, it has been estimated that for every hundred couples using with-drawal alone for a year there will be somewhere between five and fifteen inadvertent pregnancies. (This could mean, of course, that the method may be quite effective for some couples but perhaps totally ineffective for others.) One ad-vantage is that, for some, the method is easy to use and, in any event, doesn't require costly medical supervision. But in many cases it can create serious tensions for both part-ners, turning sexual relations into a sort of torment. Cer-tainly no one who is really serious about avoiding unwanted pregnancies should rely on withdrawal exclusively, but it may be helpful when used in conjunction with some addi-tional birth control method—for example, if a woman uses a vaginal spermicidal jelly at the same time.

THE RHYTHM METHOD

The **rhythm method** of family planning is sometimes called "natural birth control," "natural family planning," "fertility awareness," or "periodic abstinence." It does not involve the use of any drugs, hormones, or physical barriers; rather, it depends on imposing a barrier of *space and time* to prevent sperm from fertilizing a ripened ovum. The barrier of *space* is erected by abstaining from sexual intercourse at certain points during the woman's ovulation cycle. The barrier of *time* is imposed by controlling or confining sexual contacts to the times during the ovulation cycle when the woman is least likely to be fertile. The basic idea underlying this method is easy enough to understand. But successfully put-ting that idea into practice is not simple, and the end results do not compare at all favorably with other birth control methods. Unless a person really feels, for moral or reli-gious reasons, that the rhythm method is the *only* method of birth control available, it is usually *not* a good choice. Unfortunately, many of those who *do* feel that way may use nothing at all for birth control because they don't under-stand how the rhythm method works. For those people, we are going to discuss it in detail. Certainly for those who must use it, the rhythm method is better than nothing at all if it is used properly and intelligently.

The idea of the rhythm method arises from what we learned in chapter two about a woman's ovulation time and the time during her ovulation cycle—the *only* time—that she is fertile and able to conceive. Until a ripened ovum is released from an ovary, there is no ovum available to be fertilized. Once a fertilized ovum *is* released and moves down into a Fallopian tube, it will survive only a brief time—perhaps 48 hours at the maximum, and probably as little as 12 or 15 hours in most cases—and then will die and disintegrate *if it isn't fertilized by a sperm sometime during that brief interval.*

This means that a woman is actually fertile—able to conceive—for only about 1 or 2 days out of every month-long ovulation cycle; the rest of the time she is *in*fertile or *un*able to conceive. *If she abstains from sexual intercourse for long enough before, during, and after those particular 1 or 2 days, so that there are no sperm available to fertilize her ripened ovum during its brief time of existence, then she won't become pregnant* and can have intercourse during all the rest of her ovulation cycle without worrying about pregnancy.

In theory, that would seem to mean that if she abstained from intercourse for just a few days a month, she could have intercourse any other time she desired and never have an undesired pregnancy. But in practice it's not that simple, for two major reasons. First of all, for many women, it can be difficult to determine *exactly* when she ovulates and will therefore be fertile for a while. If she abstains from intercourse for the wrong few days, she's very likely to become pregnant, and it's hard for her to tell for certain which few days are the right ones. Second, nobody knows for certain exactly how long sperm cells, deposited in a woman's vagina during intercourse and caught up in the mucus at the cervical entrance to the womb, may survive there and retain their ability to find and fertilize a ripened ovum. But many studies indicate that those sperm may survive and remain potent (able to fertilize an ovum) for as long as 4 or 5 days. For these reasons, the rhythm method won't work reliably just by abstaining from intercourse for a select two or three days; the interval of abstention, or "no sexual contact," has to be considerably longer than that in order to include some days both *before* and *after* ovulation —and this interval of "no contact" has to be even longer yet, unless the woman has some way to determine quite accurately *when she is ovulating.*

Pinpointing Ovulation. It is possible to solve this problem, in most cases, but it takes a good deal of care, attention, and self-examination to do it. Success may depend upon several variables, including just how regular a woman's periods are. As we have seen, you can't tell when the *next* ovulation is going to take place from when the *last* menstrual period began or ended—but it *is* possible to gain some useful information about ovulation time in other ways. In fact, there are several different ways that may help you determine when you have ovulated.

1) *Keeping a calendar.* This can be a very important tool. Don't use an ordinary wall calendar, which is too clumsy for comparing one ovulation cycle with another because it is geared to days of the week and month, not to ovulation cycles. *Make your own calendar.* On a sheet of paper draw several horizontal bars divided into 32 spaces each (33 or 34 spaces if your personal cycle happens to be longer than most) with the spaces numbered 1 through 32 from left to right. Label the bars "Cycle 1," "Cycle 2," etc. (See example in figure 5.)

The numbers refer to the days of your ovulation or menstrual cycle, not the days of any month, but you may want to indicate the days of the week too, for convenience. For Day 1 of Cycle 1 you will want to pick some day that is always easily identified. Since for most women the first

Figure 5

CYCLE 1

| 1 | 2 | 3 | 4 | 5 | 6 | 7 | 8 | 9 | 10 | 11 | 12 | 13 | 14 | 15 | 16 | 17 | 18 | 19 | 20 | 21 | 22 | 23 | 24 | 25 | 26 | 27 | 28 | 29 | 30 | 31 |

CYCLE 2

| 1 | 2 | 3 | 4 | 5 | 6 | 7 | 8 | 9 | 10 | 11 | 12 | 13 | 14 | 15 | 16 | 17 | 18 | 19 | 20 | 21 | 22 | 23 | 24 | 25 | 26 | 27 | 28 | 29 | 30 | 31 |

CYCLE 3

| 1 | 2 | 3 | 4 | 5 | 6 | 7 | 8 | 9 | 10 | 11 | 12 | 13 | 14 | 15 | 16 | 17 | 18 | 19 | 20 | 21 | 22 | 23 | 24 | 25 | 26 | 27 | 28 | 29 | 30 | 31 |

CYCLE 4

| 1 | 2 | 3 | 4 | 5 | 6 | 7 | 8 | 9 | 10 | 11 | 12 | 13 | 14 | 15 | 16 | 17 | 18 | 19 | 20 | 21 | 22 | 23 | 24 | 25 | 26 | 27 | 28 | 29 | 30 | 31 |

day of a menstrual period is usually pretty definite, this may be the easiest and most reliable day to choose as Day 1. Mark that day, and each subsequent day that you have flow, with an "X." You know that you're probably going to ovulate sometime between about 8 and 15 days *after* the last day of your period, but you don't know which one yet, so all you can do at this point is make a big oval circle around the spaces for those days (i.e., around Days 14 to 21).

2) *Charting your cycles.* As you pass through those "suspect days," 14 through 21, pay special attention to see if you have a little sharp, cramping abdominal pain on one day that you don't usually have on other days. This could be the mittelschmerz we spoke of in chapter two which occurs in some women, sometimes, just a few hours before ovulation. If you have such a pain, mark a question mark in a circle in the space for the day it occurs. (In our example, let's say it was on Day 16.) Even if the timing seems right, there still has to be a question mark at this point, because the pain could come from something else. If you don't have any such pain, of course, don't mark the question mark in. A mittelschmerzlike pain is a possible clue to ovulation time that *can* be important *if* you have it regularly, at about the same time in your cycle, every month or every other month, as time goes on. If you have something of the sort only irregularly, or once every six months, these notations aren't going to help much.

The next noticeable event in the cycle will occur around Day 28, 29, or 30, a little earlier in some women, a little later in others—the first day of your next menstrual period. Whatever day of Cycle 1 that is, scratch off the Day number and mark it Day 1 and then drop down to the Cycle 2 calendar and mark your "menstruation X" in Day 1. (This means the last day of Cycle 1 overlaps the first day of Cycle 2).

Now you have something a little more definite to help you identify *when you ovulated during Cycle 1.* As we saw in chapter two, the interval between ovulation in the middle of a cycle and the beginning of the next menstrual period (assuming that fertilization has not taken place) is about 14 days in most women, pretty consistently, period after period. Therefore, you can count back 14 days and mark a question mark in the Day box 14 days before your next period started (in our example, Day 15). *That day is probably within a day or two of the day you ovulated during Cycle 1.* What is more, if you happen to have a mittelschmerz question mark in the same day box, or one close on either side, you have *double confirmation* that this is probably about when you ovulated.

So what good is this information, considering that you have already started Cycle 2? Not very much, taken all by itself—but compared to what happens in Cycle 2, and then again in Cycle 3, and so on, it can soon be very useful indeed. What you are looking for is a *reliable, regular, repeating pattern.* Suppose in Cycle 2 your menstruation goes through Day 7 (see figure 6). You don't notice anything like mittelschmerz that you can recognize, but the first day of your next menstrual period again falls on Day 29 (which becomes Day 1 of Cycle 3). Then suppose that during that Cycle 3, your period runs only 6 days and you have some twinges of abdominal pain on Day 16. And suppose your next period begins on Day 30. Counting back 14 days, you will find you are marking *two* question marks in the same Day box for Cycle 3.

3) *Estimating your fertile period.* This now begins to look promising. First of all, you have found that you are having quite regular periods. This isn't just a vague general impression—you've actually *documented* that, around Day 28 or 29, it's about time for you to begin your period, and that you are *probably* ovulating around Day 15, 16, or 17 of each cycle. Assuming that sperm discharged into the vagina any time five days or less *before* possible ovulation on Day 15 might survive long enough to fertilize the ovum, and assuming that the ovum might survive for 2 days *after*

Figure 6

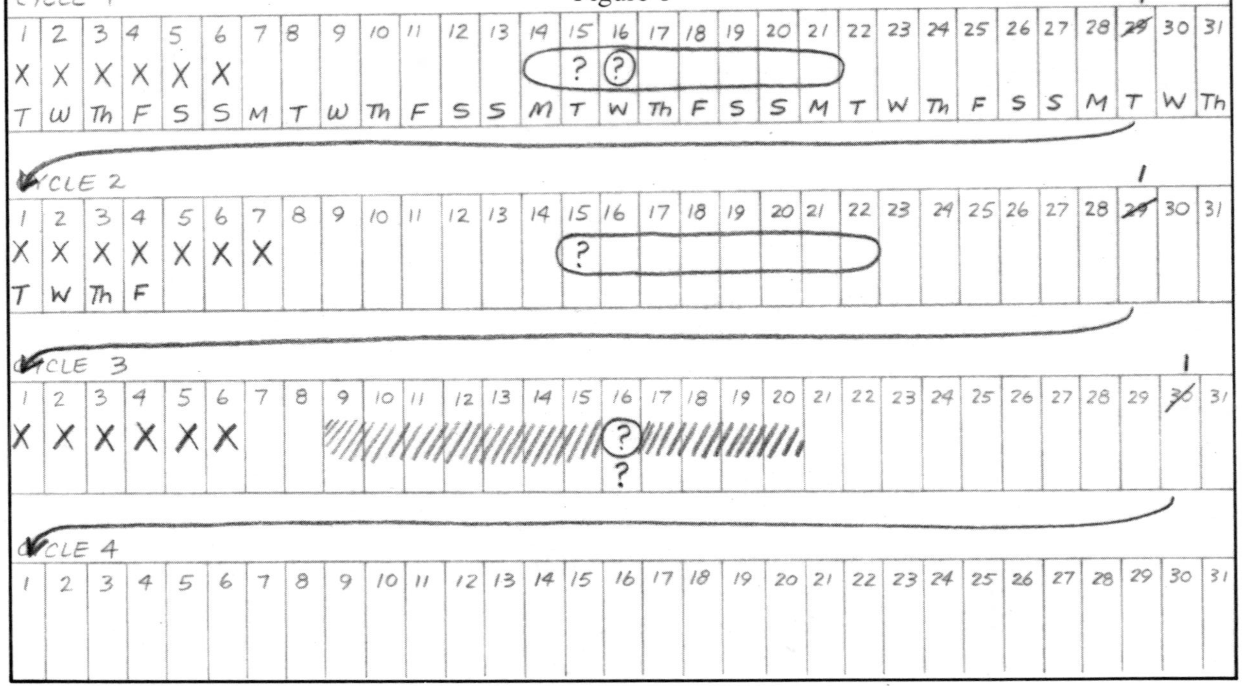

possible ovulation on Day 17, then you would have a *danger period*—a period when fertilization might possibly take place—extending from Day 10 through Day 19, and *this is the interval through which you must abstain from sexual intercourse in order for the rhythm method of birth control to work with any reliability.* It would be even safer to extend the period of no sexual intercourse a day on either end—say from Day 9 through Day 20. Thus, the "safe" days would begin on Day 21 of one cycle and extend through Day 8 of the next cycle. Add this up and we come up with:

No sex—12 days per ovulation cycle

Sex okay—17 days per ovulation cycle

All this is assuming that your ovulation and/or menstrual cycle is really quite regular and predictable—something you can determine only by maintaining your calendar faithfully for several months. Unfortunately, many teenage girls (or even older women) just *aren't* all that regular—their periods may vary in length by several days, or the whole cycle may vary in length by several days. If you find that your periods actually are *not* very regular and predictable, this method of birth control is not likely to work for you, and you should consider using a more reliable method. You should also *completely abstain from intercourse* (or use a condom or diaphragm) during the months while you are setting up your calendar. Finally, some women just *don't* ovulate a neat 14 days before the beginning of a period—in fact, in some women, ovulation *may* occur almost any time during the menstrual cycle, at least sometimes, and maybe (in rare cases) even in the middle of a menstrual period. Clearly, even if your periods are very regular and predictable, you need something else to help you pinpoint your ovulation time more accurately.

4) *Charting basal body temperature* is that "something else." This means *actually taking your temperature at the same time each day and writing it down on your calen-*

dar. Ordinarily, if you don't have a fever from some infection, and aren't overheated from heavy exercise, you will find that your body temperature will be essentially the same each day at a given time, within 1/10° F. or so, if you measure it with a thermometer. This holds true except for one time during the month, for a woman: usually, a few hours after she ovulates, her basal body temperature will *increase* between 1/2° and 1° F., and that elevation will continue daily for several days after ovulation before gradually going back down again.

This increase in basal body temperature can be a remarkably reliable signal that ovulation has occurred. The temperature change isn't great, but it's enough in most women to notice it—if the woman measures her basal temperature faithfully, day after day, at the same time every day. Usually the best time for measurement is when you first awaken in the morning, before you get up and begin heating up your body by stirring around, and before eating, drinking, or smoking. (Bedtime or any other time is okay, too, as long as it's the same time every day and you haven't had anything to eat, drink, or smoke for an hour before taking it.) An oral (under the tongue) temperature measurement is fine. Read the thermometer to the nearest 1/10 of a degree after it's been under your tongue for three full minutes and mark the temperature down on your calendar. On the day you find your basal temperature increased by 1/2° or more from the previous level, mark that Day box on your calendar with an "ovulation question mark."

If the temperature change is definite, this is probably as close as you are going to come to pinpointing your exact time of ovulation—the day of the temperature change or the day before. If this day agrees with your "mittelschmerz" day (if you have one) and/or with the "14-days-before-the-next-period" day, and the same thing occurs on the same day two or three months in a row, then you are probably really focused in on your ovulation time and can change the question mark to an exclamation point. But if this day *varies* from the other signals, and does so consistently for two or three months running, you should count more heavily on the temperature-change day than on the other signals because it is far more likely to be right for *you*.

5) *Cervical mucus.* One other signal of ovulation *may* be useful for *some* women, if they are able to observe it. Approximately a day before ovulation, the hormones in the woman's body produce a change in the amount and stretchiness of the mucus around the cervix. Usually that mucus is scant, rather thick, and forms a sort of obstructing plug in the cervix—but just prior to ovulation, the mucus becomes thinner, more copious, and more stringy or stretchy than normal—the better to allow sperm to find their way through to the Fallopian tube. Many obstetrician/gynecologists, or many Planned Parenthood or birth control clinics, teach women how to sample their cervical mucus (using a finger or a tongue depressor) and then test it between their fingers for slipperiness and stretchiness, and some women can learn to detect the change that occurs just before ovulation, thus adding one more signal you can chart to help corroborate the day that you ovulate.

By fine-tuning the probable ovulation day by these various methods, many women can pin their ovulation time down to about two days. Then, by planning to abstain from sexual intercourse for 6 days prior to the first of those two days, and for 3 days after the second, they can end up with just a 10- or 11-day period of abstention. They then have at their command a relatively effective method of avoiding undesired pregnancies—as long as they actually *do* abstain during the necessary interval of time.

Advantages of the Rhythm Method. For couples who are highly motivated to avoid unwanted pregnancy, who fully understand the method, and are willing to devote the necessary care and attention to achieve that goal, the rhythm method can provide a good, reliable form of birth control. (See *Effectiveness of the Rhythm Method* on page 64.) It can be particularly effective when the woman's ovulation cycles and menstrual periods are very regular and predictable, without much variation from cycle to cycle. For these couples, it provides a "natural" form of birth control that meets the approval of Roman Catholic teachings—and since it doesn't involve medications or mechanical devices that have to be purchased, it can be very inexpensive as well. And, of course, it is completely reversible—just discontinue abstaining during your fertile days and pregnancy will occur according to normal patterns. Finally, because it requires a great deal of openness, communication, and mutual forbearance on the part of the couples, it may contribute to a stronger overall sexual relationship and a greater sense of mutual sharing in a marriage.

Disadvantages of the Rhythm Method. Probably the major disadvantage of this method of birth control is that it isn't really "natural" at all—it imposes some very rigid and unnatural limitations upon when a couple may or may not have sexual intercourse, and both partners must agree to abide by those limitations, like it or not, or it isn't going to work. Many couples find it extremely difficult to regiment their sex lives with one eye on the calendar and the other on a thermometer. Many feel that it forces their sex relationship to lose spontaneity— as indeed it must during more than one third of every cycle. Under such physical or emotional pressures, many couples counting on this method for protection may at least occasionally throw caution to the winds, deciding at the last moment to "take a chance this time"—and when that happens they immediately *don't have any protection at all.* It is the likelihood of this kind of "chance taking" which has led some people to speak of the rhythm method rather disparagingly as "Vatican Roulette."

The second big disadvantage is that when you lose at roulette, you *lose*—you can't take things back later or undo what you've done. The two people committed to "natural" birth control methods *don't have any backup when they make a mistake*—unless they abandon their "natural" birth control philosophy. As we will see later, with other forms of birth control—barrier methods, for instance—there are things to fall back on when the primary birth control method fails for some reason—but not with "natural" birth control. For this reason, and because sexual impulses may be very unpredictable, the woman who *absolutely mustn't* have an accidental pregnancy should not rely on the rhythm method or any other "natural method."

A third disadvantage is that, for some women, using the rhythm method effectively is very difficult or impossible because of illness, irregular periods, spontaneously missed periods, or other menstrual or ovulation disorders. Such a woman can have a terrible time figuring out when she's probably ovulating and when she's not, even with expert advice guiding her—and if she really, sincerely, wants to prevent unwanted pregnancies, she shouldn't use this method. *Even a woman who is quite regular and predictable should have the guidance of an obstetrician or gynecologist, or of birth control experts at a Planned Parenthood clinic or other birth control facility, when she first undertakes the rhythm method*—simply because there can be a good deal of individual variation, and because expert, hands-on guidance and support is extremely important until you really know what you're doing with this method.

A final disadvantage is simply the time it takes to set up a calendar and get used to charting basal temperatures and so forth—an interval of perhaps months during which the woman just isn't effectively protected against pregnancy. Of course, a young woman who hasn't yet become sexually active can start preparing to use the rhythm method, with the kind of medical guidance mentioned above, and learn all about identifying her own ovulation time before she ever has intercourse—if the motivation and family support are there. Otherwise, she, or any other woman intending to use this method, should either abstain from sex and/or use some alternative birth control (such as condoms or a diaphragm, both of which won't interfere with setting up a calendar and charting temperatures) until she has already charted several periods, found out how the rhythm method will work for *her*, and is ready to practice it.

Effectiveness of the Rhythm Method. Unfortunately, there is no good way to tell in advance how effective—or ineffective—the rhythm method will be for any given couple, partly because there is so much variation in how effectively different couples use the method. But most authorities on birth control believe that, for people using the rhythm method exclusively, the overall risk of unwanted pregnancy is quite high, ranging from 10 to 20 percent—that is, between 10 and 20 pregnancies for every hundred women using the method exclusively for a year. This failure rate compares so poorly with most other birth control methods that the rhythm method simply doesn't make sense for anyone except those who feel, for moral or religious reasons, that they can't use any other method. And it is important for those people to realize that the rhythm method is *not* an easy, casual, or hassle-free method of birth control. If you want to use it, and want it to work, you have to *make* it work.

EXTENDED NURSING

One other "natural" form of birth control isn't really "birth control" at all, per se, but simply a side effect of another natural process—nursing a baby. During the latter stages of pregnancy a hormone known as **prolactin** stimulates enlargement of the woman's breasts, so that when the baby is born, milk flow will begin within a few hours. When the baby then nurses, the nipple and breast stimulation of the nursing triggers short, intense bursts of prolactin production in the mother, so as to ensure continuing milk production. But one other effect of high prolactin levels in the mother's bloodstream is to *inhibit* production of the hormones that would normally trigger a new ovulation, so that while the mother continues nursing, ovulation tends to be postponed. And, of course, as long as ovulation is postponed, a ripened ovum isn't formed and the woman doesn't become pregnant.

Thus, after delivering a baby, a nursing mother will enjoy a period free of ovulation considerably longer than if she were bottle-feeding the baby, and this ovulation-free interval can be extended to some degree by extended nursing. Nursing a baby indefinitely is by no means a perfect guarantee that ovulation won't occur, but it has been found that in societies where all mothers nurse their babies exclusively for prolonged intervals—up to two or two-and-a-half years—ovulation and new pregnancies generally don't occur until the nursing is stopped.

It might seem, then, that any mother who continued extended nursing might have effective "birth control" for as long as she nursed. Unfortunately, this doesn't work in all cases. Prolactin doesn't last long in the bloodstream; in order to effectively suppress ovulation, new bursts of prolactin have to be triggered by nursing over and over again, even in the course of the same day, and during the night as well. To be effective for preventing ovulation, the woman must be nursing the baby *exclusively* and *frequently*, without using supplemental bottle feedings, and the effect is likely to be lost once the baby starts taking a "long sleep" during the night. Finally, many modern mothers don't want to continue nursing their babies quite that frequently for such prolonged intervals. Thus, whereas extended nursing *could* be used as a long-term birth control method following birth of a baby, most women will presently find it unreliable and would just as soon resume some other less demanding form of birth control after a couple of months.

5

BARRIER METHODS
OF BIRTH CONTROL

The rhythm method of birth control discussed in the last chapter imposes a barrier of time and space between the ripened ovum and the sperm by timing and spacing intercourse so that it occurs only when there is no ripened ovum available to fertilize. Barrier methods of birth control work by imposing an actual *physical* barrier to separate the sperm cells from the ripened ovum so that the sperm cells cannot reach it.

This barrier may be *mechanical*—an impenetrable sheet of rubber, for example, in the case of a condom or diaphragm, or a vaginal film or vaginal sponge. Or it may be a *chemical* barrier composed of sperm-killing compounds mixed into a gel or foam for use in the vagina. In order for either type of barrier to be the most effective and reliable in actual use, both types of barrier are usually used simultaneously.

Compared to the rhythm method, which requires careful advance planning, identification of ovulation time as closely as possible, and abstention from intercourse for relatively long intervals during the ovulation cycle, barrier methods of birth control are handy, quick, and easy to use whenever the occasion arises, whether the woman happens to be fertile at the moment or not. But, as with any birth control method, barrier methods must be used *correctly* in order to be effective.

Since spermicidal preparations are sometimes (although unwisely) used as the *only* barrier between sperm and ovum, and since they are an important *addition* to help make condoms or diaphragms more effective, let's consider the use of spermicides first.

SPERMICIDAL
(CHEMICAL) BARRIERS

A **spermicide** is a drug or chemical which will kill sperm cells on contact. Various chemicals have been used in the past, including quite powerful acids and mercury compounds, but these have been discarded because of possible long-term health hazards. Most modern spermicidal preparations today contain high concentrations of a safe and effective compound known as **Nonoxynol-9,** which kills sperm. Nonoxynol-9 is mixed into some sort of base substance, usually a gel or a cream, which can be inserted into the vagina. There it spreads quickly to coat the inner surface of the vagina as well as the cervix, so that ejaculated sperm will immediately come in contact with the sperm-killing chemical. A newer spermicide known as Menfegol has been used for some years in Japan and other countries but is not yet available in the United States.

Spermicides can be purchased over the counter (i.e., without a doctor's prescription) at drugstores and in several different forms:

1) *Vaginal suppositories or vaginal inserts.* These are small, bullet-shaped tablets containing the spermicide in a dissolvable base. A suppository inserted into the vagina a few minutes before intercourse will dissolve and spread the spermicide to coat the vaginal canal and cervix. Some sup-

positories contain a foaming agent which releases tiny bubbles of carbon dioxide as the insert melts. This foam helps to spread the spermicide quickly and also provides a network of bubbles to trap the sperm.

2) *Creams and jellies.* These preparations come in tubes, usually packed with a syringelike applicator. A syringe full of a cream of jelly can be withdrawn from the tube, using the syringe applicator, and then inserted high up in the vagina before intercourse. (See figure 7.) Creams or jellies melt quickly at body temperature. Either can also be used for thoroughly coating the outside of a condom after it has been put on, or for coating both sides of a diaphragm before insertion.

3) *Foaming aerosols.* These work on the same principle as the foaming suppositories, but the bubbles are formed by gas under pressure in the aerosol can—much like foaming shaving cream. Again, a syringe applicator is filled from the container, and the foam is then inserted in the vagina before intercourse.

Advantages of spermicidal preparations. These preparations are relatively inexpensive and readily available at any drugstore, with instructions for use included with each package. They are handy and quick to use when the occasion demands and small enough to carry in a purse or even a clutch bag. You use them only when you need them, and they are there when you need them. There are no lasting side effects, and there is no interference with the woman's fertility.

Disadvantages of spermicidal preparations. Many people find them messy to use, and there is some vaginal discharge after intercourse. None of them taste very good, a concern for those who engage in oral stimulation as part of sex relations. Furthermore, an application of a spermicide is good for just one episode of intercourse—if another engagement follows later, the spermicide must first be reapplied.

The main disadvantage, however, is that spermicides

USING A SYRINGE APPLICATOR TO INSERT A SPERMICIDE

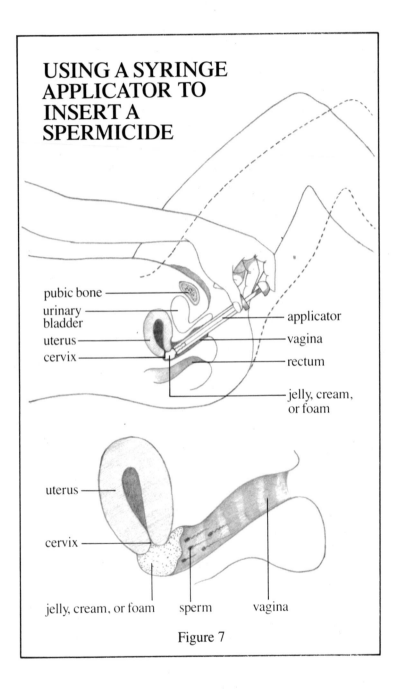

pubic bone

urinary bladder

uterus

cervix

applicator

vagina

rectum

jelly, cream, or foam

uterus

cervix

jelly, cream, or foam   sperm   vagina

Figure 7

aren't very effective as the *only* birth control method. When sperm are ejaculated close to the uterine cervix, it takes only an instant for some of them to penetrate into the safety of the cervical mucus and make their way up out of reach of the spermicide. Thus, for women using spermicides alone, there will be somewhere between 10 and 20 pregnancies per 100 women per year—really a very poor record if you are seriously trying to avoid pregnancy. This might be improved somewhat if the couple were to use a spermicidal preparation in combination with *coitus interruptus*, but the risk would still be quite high. By far the best and most effective use of spermicidal preparations is in conjunction with some additional barrier method—the use of either a condom or a diaphragm.

THE CONDOM

The **condom,** or **penile sheath,** is a tubular device, closed at one end, which can be rolled down over the erect penis before the penis is inserted into the vagina during intercourse. (See figure 8.) The most popular (and least expensive) condoms in use today are made of very thin, stretchable latex rubber with a small reservoir at the closed end to receive and hold the ejaculated semen. These condoms are quality-tested, using either air pressure or water pressure, to ensure against pinhole flaws or breakage. And, while breakage *may* occur during use, this occurs very rarely. Most such condoms come prelubricated and pre-rolled, to make them easy to put on, and are sealed in individual foil or plastic wrappers. They are intended to be used once and then discarded after sex. Some such condoms today are available in various colors, and some have ribbing or other texturing on the outside. Such refinements may make them more attractive to some people but of course have no influence on their effectiveness.

Condoms are intended to be used just once and then discarded after sex. They prevent pregnancy by keeping the man's sperm out of the woman's vagina during sex. But to do this, they have to be used in the right way. Here are some "condom sense" rules for using a condom correctly:*

(1) Use a condom *every single time* you have sex.
(2) The man should put the condom on as soon as his penis is erect, before he has *any* contact with the woman's vulva or vagina.
(3) Roll the condom all the way down to the base of the penis before starting sex. (See figure 8.)
(4) Coat the condom with a spermicidal jelly or foam before sex. This will make the outside slippery and keep the condom from tearing. *Don't* use vaseline or vegetable oil for this. These things make the rubber break down.
(5) The man should pull his penis out soon after climax, before it gets soft, holding onto the rim of the condom so it doesn't slip off. That way sperm can't accidentally spill into the vagina.
(6) Don't use the same condom more than once.
(7) To be extra safe, the woman should also put a spermicide into her vagina before sex. This combination of a spermicide and a condom used together gives very good protection against getting pregnant.

Advantages of condom use. There are a great many advantages which account for the widespread popularity of this birth control device. Condoms are inexpensive and readily available in any drugstore without any doctor's prescription. Their use is self-evident, so no medical appointment or doctor's instructions are required. They are convenient—easy for the man or woman to carry and have available at a mo-

*Adapted from Hatcher, Robert. *Contraceptive Technology 1986–1987*, ed. 13. New York: Irvington Publishers, 1987; and Goldsmith, Marsha F. "Medical News and Perspectives," *Journal of the American Medical Association*, May 1, 1987, Vol. 257, No. 17.

APPLYING A CONDOM

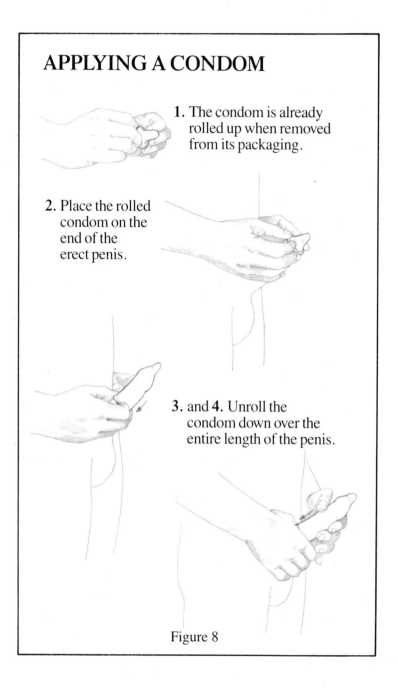

1. The condom is already rolled up when removed from its packaging.

2. Place the rolled condom on the end of the erect penis.

3. and 4. Unroll the condom down over the entire length of the penis.

Figure 8

ment's notice. And they have a long shelf (or pocket) life; as long as they remain in their original wrappers, condoms will not deteriorate for many months (although heat can damage them, and one carried around in a pocket or purse should probably be replaced every year).

Furthermore, the condom is one birth control method that is largely under control of the *man*, and, even if required infrequently, it doesn't require a lot of advance preparation. It is ideally suited for individuals, male or female, who have irregular, changing, or sporadic sexual relationships—for those, for example, who simply don't know, from one week to the next, whether they are going to have a sexual encounter or not. This, of course, makes the condom singularly well suited to the life-styles of single, relatively unattached young men, or for sexually active teenage girls who have no other protection against pregnancy.

Finally, the condom has one additional very important advantage in these days of uncertain sexual relationships and the proliferation of such sexually transmitted diseases as gonorrhea, genital herpes, or AIDS: it protects against infection, whether from bacteria or viruses. Indeed, condoms have been strongly recommended for servicemen by military health authorities ever since World War II, primarily as protection, or **prophylaxis,** against sexually transmitted diseases—the reason they are still today sometimes called *prophylactics.* (Incidentally, spermicidal gels and other such preparations alone do *not* have this protective advantage—they may kill sperm cells, but they cannot be counted on to kill bacteria or viruses).

Disadvantages of condom use. The main disadvantage of the condom—and the main reason for its reputation for frequent failures—is that it *has to be put on, and put on at the right time, in order to work.* Once the man's penis is erect, the condom is simply rolled down the whole length of the shaft to the base. (See figure 8.) This means that the foreplay, before intercourse begins, must be interrupted at just the point where it may have become very difficult to do so. For couples who regularly use condoms, placing the sheath on the man's penis is often regarded as just an additional form of foreplay—but many couples find it interruptive or intrusive.

Another disadvantage is that, at least occasionally, sperm may inadvertently get into the woman's vagina in spite of condom use. This can happen even before ejaculation, as we have seen, if sexual contact begins before the condom is put in place. In other cases, there can be some leakage of semen around the base of the penis, particularly if sexual contact continues for some time after ejaculation. Finally, there is the extremely rare instance in which the condom breaks, either during extremely vigorous intercourse, or because it has been snagged by a fingernail during placement, or else has some manufacturing flaw. In any of these instances, good "backup coverage" is supplied if the condom is being used in conjunction with a vaginal spermicide, and except for outright total breakage of the device, the spermicide may cover the situation. In the event of such breakage, if it is really imperative to prevent pregnancy, the woman may need to consult a doctor about a "morning after" contraceptive for backup, as discussed in chapter seven.

Effectiveness of condom use. Casual use—or misuse—of the condom alone doesn't have a very good reputation for effectiveness; lots of failures seem to occur. In most cases, this happens when the condom isn't actually used at all, or is put on too late, after sexual contact begins, as a sort of an afterthought. In such cases, use of the condom alone may have a high failure rate. But when the condom is used intelligently, as discussed above, and in conjunction with a vaginal spermicide, couples using this method can achieve protection at the rate of only 1 to 3 pregnancies per 100 women per year—an effectiveness that compares favorably with the Pill or the intrauterine device. Thus, effectiveness here is mostly a matter of paying attention and doing things right.

THE DIAPHRAGM

Before the advent of the Pill, the vaginal **diaphragm** was perhaps the single most widely used birth control method in this country, and its popularity continues today as a safe, convenient, and readily available barrier-type birth control method.

With the condom, the physical barrier is a thin latex rubber sheath enclosing the penis and preventing sperm from escaping into the vagina. As such, it is used by the male partner. The diaphragm is the female counterpart: a round, latex rubber dome which is inserted into the vagina before intercourse and which covers the upper end of the vagina and the cervical opening into the uterus, preventing sperm discharged into the vagina from entering the cervical canal and thus from reaching the ripened ovum in the Fallopian tube.

Modern diaphragms range from about 3 to 4 inches (40 to 70 mm) in diameter. The rolled edge, or circumference, of the diaphragm contains a rather firm, round, steel spring which, when released, maintains a firm round edge. (See figure 9.) But when opposite edges of the diaphragm are compressed, the device forms a tube rather the size and shape of a tampon which can easily be inserted with the fingers high up into the vagina. Then, when released, the spring expands into a firm circle again. The upper back edge (the edge closest to the spine) fits high up in the vault of the vagina behind the cervix. The front edge fits up under the ledge of the pubic bone in front, thus stretching the dome of the diaphragm over the entire cervix. Proper placement of the diaphragm is shown in figure 9.

Ordinarily, a diaphragm should be fitted by a physician or the office nurse in order to determine the right size for the individual user. The springs in different diaphragms

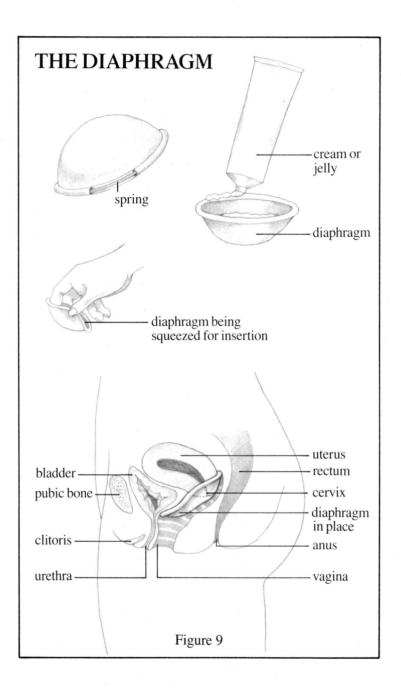

THE DIAPHRAGM

spring

cream or jelly

diaphragm

diaphragm being squeezed for insertion

bladder
pubic bone
clitoris
urethra

uterus
rectum
cervix
diaphragm in place
anus
vagina

Figure 9

vary slightly—some have just a coiled steel ring, which compresses into a tube, while others have a slightly different spring which compresses into a narrow, boat-shaped configuration for insertion. These differences are intended to meet slight variations in the individual woman's anatomy. The doctor will recommend and prescribe a specific size and type of diaphragm suitable for the individual patient, and then he or she (or, often, an experienced office nurse) will give the woman specific instructions for inserting the device and will then check to see that she is inserting it properly. Because of this need for fitting and instruction, diaphragms are available on a doctor's prescription only.

Inserting the diaphragm. It isn't *hard* to insert a diaphragm properly, but it takes a certain knack, so you should practice with supervision until you're sure you've got it right. *First, the diaphragm should be coated generously with a spermicidal jelly or cream on both sides.* Probably half the effectiveness of the diaphragm depends on this step, so it should never be neglected. In addition to providing added protection, the jelly or cream will provide lubrication for insertion. Many women find it easiest to then stand with one foot on the floor and the other on a chair or toilet seat while inserting. Others find it easier to insert while lying back on a bed with the legs spread. Whichever position suits you best, pinch the opposite edges of the spermicide-coated diaphragm together with thumb and forefinger and insert it *upward and backward* as far into the vagina as your fingers will reach. At this point the spring will have released into a circle. Find the forward edge of the spring and tuck it up onto the ledge of the pubic bone in front, just inside the upper side of the vagina. If the diaphragm is properly fitted and placed, as in figure 9, you shouldn't even be able to feel it inside after a moment, and it should stay securely in position, without any sensation of being there, throughout intercourse. (The man doesn't feel it either.) When the time comes to remove it, simply push the upper edge of the diaphragm down from the pubic ledge and extract it. Don't worry about it "getting lost" or not being able to remove it—taking it out is even simpler than putting it in.

The diaphragm can be put in place any time from minutes to an hour or so before intercourse. (If it remains in place much longer than that before intercourse, some additional spermicide should be placed in the vagina before sex begins.) After intercourse, the diaphragm should be *left in place undisturbed for a minimum of 6 hours before removal* —overnight is just fine. If there is repeated intercourse, leave the diaphragm untouched but use additional spermicidal jelly in the vagina before each entry, and then wait at least 6 hours after the *last* contact. At that point, or at least the next day, remove the diaphragm, wash it carefully, dry it, inspect it for any pinholes or tears, and store it in a clean, dry place in the case it came in. *Don't* leave it in place indefinitely, no matter how sexually active you are. Every doctor occasionally sees a novice diaphragm user complaining of a copious, foul-smelling vaginal discharge and discovers that the woman hasn't removed her diaphragm for six weeks.

Advantages of diaphragm use. The diaphragm is handy, inexpensive, easy to have available at a moment's notice, and its use is entirely under the control of the woman—she doesn't have to count on anybody else to do anything. Properly fitted, properly inserted, and used with a spermicidal jelly or cream, the diaphragm offers highly effective birth control protection, with fewer than 3 or 4 failures per 100 women per year. Although it takes a little initial instruction and a little practice to learn to insert it, it then becomes extremely easy to use. It doesn't require any hormones or other drugs to be taken internally, nor any procedure to follow during times when a woman is sexually inactive, and of course it is completely and instantly reversible any time a pregnancy is desired—no "waiting period." Nor does the diaphragm have any ill effect on a woman's fertility—it is a *temporary barrier to sperm*, nothing more. Unlike the condom, which is generally discarded after one use, the diaphragm should last for a couple of years if it is handled and treated gently. Most authorities recommend replacing it after two years, simply because latex rubber does begin to deteriorate with time.

Disadvantages of diaphragm use. As with the condom, the diaphragm has to be used in order to work—it will not protect you if it is sitting in a dresser drawer. If it is improperly fitted (i.e., too small) it may slip around inside and allow sperm to leak past it—a problem at least partially offset by coating it liberally on both sides with spermicide— or (if too large) it may feel uncomfortable and/or lead to urinary distress or bladder infections. (If you gain or lose a good deal of weight, the fit of the diaphragm may also change and should be checked by a doctor.) Also, as with the condom, a diaphragm can interrupt the spontaneity of the sex act if you wait to insert it until the last minute— but, for some, it may seem "cold and calculating" to insert it well in advance, especially if you feel that sex is best when it "just happens." But, considering that virtually *any* birth control method is going to exact *some* price, of *some* sort, *some*where, this price may not be too great.

Effectiveness of diaphragm use. As we noted above, the diaphragm can be highly effective when used properly with the additional backup of a spermicidal preparation. Because it sometimes isn't used that way, or is used only sporadically, or removed too soon, it has a somewhat unfair reputation for unreliability, leading to the saying that "there's a baby in every diaphragm." In practice, however, multitudes of couples use the diaphragm exclusively for birth control protection year after year, with no failures whatever, and they interrupt the method only when children are desired. Generally, a diaphragm should be refitted after a baby is born, however, because of changes that may have occurred in the woman's anatomy as a result of childbirth. The diaphragm is especially useful as an "in between" birth control method when a woman who ordinarily uses the Pill drops off for a while, or for an interval of time immediately after childbirth, or when only a temporary birth control method is desired.

THE VAGINAL SPONGE

A comparative newcomer among birth control methods, the vaginal sponge combines both mechanical and chemical barriers in one but has yet to prove itself as far as convenience, safety, and effectiveness are concerned. Essentially, this device is a small sponge impregnated with Nonoxynol-9 spermicide. After moistening, it is inserted high up in the woman's vagina before intercourse. During sex, the sponge is pressed up to fill the top of the vaginal vault and cover the cervix, with spermicide to kill the sperm released at ejaculation, while the spongelike material forms a mechanical barrier to sperm. As with a diaphragm, the sponge should be left in place for 6 hours after intercourse. Then it should be removed and disposed of.

During clinical testing, the vaginal sponge was found to have a high degree of effectiveness—about equal to that of the diaphragm—but was much easier to insert. Since a proper fitting is unnecessary, the device is available quite inexpensively, over the counter, at drugstores.

Only time will tell whether the vaginal sponge will maintain this high effectiveness record in widespread use. But, meanwhile, a question of safety has been raised. During the early 1980s a number of women began developing **toxic shock syndrome,** or **TSS,** a dangerous group of symptoms, including fever, sore throat, skin rash, nausea or vomiting, and collapse, caused by poisons, or toxins, produced by certain kinds of staph bacteria growing in the vagina and elsewhere. Growth of the poison-producing bacteria is believed to be promoted by prolonged wearing of superabsorbent tampons which have been withdrawn from sale since TSS appeared. Although TSS is very rare, there has been some concern that it might possibly be related to use of vaginal sponge contraceptives as well. Anyone using a vaginal sponge should carefully read the manufacturer's information enclosed in the package and follow instructions for removal of the sponges after use.

FALSE IDEAS
ABOUT BIRTH CONTROL

Two very widespread mistaken ideas about birth control deserve to be mentioned here. The first has to do with douching—rinsing out the vagina with water, diluted vinegar or other solutions—immediately after intercourse. The widespread notion that this can serve as an effective protection against pregnancy is simply not true. It's not hard to see why. By the time a woman can get to the bathroom for a douche, sperm will already have penetrated the cervical mucus and started on their way up through the uterus toward their target. And any time a spermicidal preparation has been used, douching should be deliberately *postponed* until at least six hours after intercourse; if it is done any earlier, there is the possibility that the douche will wash away the spermicide while leaving some live sperm in the vagina.

Another false idea is that a woman must "come," or have a sexual climax, or **orgasm,** during intercourse in order to transport sperm up into the uterus and make fertilization possible. *Don't believe this folktale.* The notion that a female orgasm is accompanied by sufficient contraction of the uterus to suck sperm up into the tubes has been disproved —the sperm can get up there just fine on their own. A woman's orgasm doesn't have any effect whatever on fertilization or becoming pregnant.

6

THE PILL

Since it was first introduced in the 1960s, "the Pill" has become one of the most widely used birth control methods in history. Today, around 10 million women use the Pill exclusively for birth control in the United States alone, and there are some 60 million users worldwide.

It isn't hard to see why. Of all birth control methods available, hormone birth control using the Pill is by far the simplest, most convenient, hassle-free, reliable, and effective birth control method in existence. It can be used for years on end, yet is reversible within a short while any time a pregnancy is desired. It completely separates the birth control *method* from the sex act itself, so that there is no interference with sexual spontaneity, no need to *do something special* just before intercourse. The Pill is a birth control method which, for all intents and purposes, takes care of itself, so that—aside from taking the pills at the right times —the Pill user just doesn't have to worry about her protection against unwanted pregnancy.

Even so, the Pill is not a birth control panacea. There are certain problems involved with its use, and it is not suitable for all women at all times. To see how the Pill works, and how many of the problems and worries about its use have been resolved, we need to look back to history for a moment.

DISCOVERY OF THE PILL

Since ancient times women have dreamed of some medicine they could take that would protect them from becoming pregnant when they didn't want to be—but nothing ever worked until about forty years ago.

Then, in 1937, researchers discovered that if rabbits were given large doses of the female sex hormone **progesterone** (one of the two main female hormones) throughout their ovulation cycles, they would cease to ovulate. Obviously, if no ripened ovum were released from the ovary, fertilization and pregnancy could not occur. This seemed to occur in other animal species, too. The question immediately arose whether this might also hold true in humans.

Unfortunately, this was hard to determine. For one thing, natural progesterone was extremely difficult and expensive to manufacture and had to be injected daily because, when it was taken by mouth, digestive juices would break it down before it could be absorbed into the bloodstream.

Then, in 1949, an American chemist named Russell Marker found a way to extract progesterone from the roots of wild Mexican yams. Soon after, scientists at the University of Pennsylvania succeeded in making a synthetic progesterone, or **progestogen** (a laboratory-made hormone), based on the Mexican yam hormone molecule. Later, synthetic estrogens were also manufactured. These synthetic hormones could be taken effectively by mouth because they were not destroyed in the stomach. Once they were absorbed, the body responded to them just as if they were natural progesterone or estrogen. These synthetic hormones then became the basis for modern oral contraceptive pills, now known collectively as "the Pill." (One of the first companies to manufacture and distribute oral contraceptives even took its name from the words *synt*hesis and M*exi*co; today the Syntex Corporation is a major manufacturer of oral contraceptives and other drugs, with $1 *billion* worth of sales per year.)

Although synthetic progestogens alone seemed to suppress ovulation, a combination of progestogens with synthetic estrogens was found to work even better as an oral contraceptive. Taken in combination, these hormones were tested first on animals and then on human volunteers. The first human tests were extremely promising: *not one* of the women tested ovulated or became pregnant while taking the drugs. In the late 1950s much more widespread tests were conducted among women in the city of Boston and in Puerto Rico. Results were so successful—fewer than 1 to 3 pregnancies per 100 women per year—that in 1960 the U.S. Food and Drug Administration approved the combination pills for use, and widespread use of "the Pill" began.

EARLY PILLS
AND EARLY PROBLEMS

One reason the Pill became so popular so quickly was that it was so easy to use. A woman would begin taking one combination pill per day on the first day of a normal menstrual period and then continue for 21 days. Then she would discontinue the Pill for 7 days. At the end of this time, normally, she would have what appeared to be a normal menstrual period—except that there had been no ovulation. The estrogens and progesterone, acting together, *interrupted* the normal cyclic interaction of estrogen, follicle-stimulating hormone, and progesterone, with the end result that no follicle in the ovary was stimulated and no ovum was ripened and released during that cycle.

After 7 days off the Pill, the woman would again begin taking the combined pill once a day for the next 21 days, then off 7, and so forth. As long as she continued this sequential dosage of the Pill month after month, she never ovulated and thus couldn't become pregnant no matter when in her cycle she had intercourse. Best of all, she didn't have to do *anything at all* except take the Pill at the right time in order to escape the threat of pregnancy—no keeping a calendar, no forced abstention from intercourse, no inserting a diaphragm beforehand, no pausing while the man put on a condom—no nothing. The Pill caught on quickly, and by 1965 was the leading form of contraception in America.

It did its job admirably well, too, preventing pregnancy in some 98 out of 100 users. But certain problems appeared. Those early pills contained quite high doses of synthetic estrogen—as much as 150 or 200 micrograms (a microgram is one millionth of a gram) per pill—and this was enough to cause some untoward side effects. Some women starting the Pill had some swelling and tenderness of the breasts. Others had trouble with nausea or headaches. Perhaps the most troublesome direct side effect was the matter of breakthrough bleeding. A number of women first starting the Pill experienced vaginal spotting or bleeding a week or so after starting the medicine—sometimes enough to be confused with the beginning of their next menstrual period —and in some cases this "breakthrough bleeding" would occur each month on the medication. In most such women this problem became less severe after they had been on the Pill for several months—and later it became clear that the high dose of estrogen in those early pills was at least partly to blame. As pills were manufactured with lower and lower doses of estrogens, the problem became less frequent or troublesome.

Other possible side effects, however, were more worrisome. As early as 1961, medical centers began accumulating evidence that some women taking the Pill were more likely than normal to develop blood clots (known as **throm-**

boses) in their veins. In 1968 a number of studies confirmed this evidence. Other studies suggested that older women taking the Pill were more likely than normal to have strokes or heart attacks, again as a result of blood clots, and these problems seemed especially threatening among pill users who were cigarette smokers. Finally, medical researchers began to raise questions about the possibility (never demonstrated or proved) that the Pill might, over a long time, contribute to the development of breast cancer or other cancers.

These findings produced something of a scare during the late 1960s and early 1970s; many women began having second thoughts about the long-term safety of the Pill, and many stopped using it, either in favor of other birth control methods, or no birth control at all. But further studies quieted many of these fears. For one thing, the frequency of side effects seemed very much related to the dosage of hormones in the pills being used, and researchers found that ovulation could be blocked with much smaller doses of hormone, especially of the estrogen. Soon the amount of estrogen in combination pills was dropped from the original 150 micrograms per pill to 75 and then 50 micrograms per pill, with no change in contraceptive effectiveness, and many of the side effects disappeared. Modern-day pills now normally contain only about 30 micrograms of estrogen; any dosage much below that low level will no longer be fully effective in blocking ovulation.

Out of all of this experience, a great deal has been learned. Even on high-dosage pills, the number of women suffering from blood clotting and related problems was always very low and is now much lower on the low-dosage pills. Most authorities today believe that oral contraceptives are by far the safest form of contraception for young, healthy women but that the risks may outweigh the benefits in certain groups of older women. Furthermore, today we recognize certain so-called risk factors for trouble with the

Pill, and women who have one or more of those risk factors should avoid using the Pill. We will list these risk factors on pages 95-96.

THE MODERN PILL

Today there are three basic kinds of pill in use—the combination, or sequential, pills, the so-called phasic pills, and the so-called mini-pills (progesterone-only pills). The combination pills contain the same fixed amount of estrogen and progesterone in each pill, with the estrogen held to a maximum of about 30 micrograms per pill. These pills are taken in a sequence, one daily for 21 days, then discontinued for 7 days. Usually they are provided in 21-pill packets so the user knows when to stop, but some manufacturers provide "blank" or sugar pills without any hormone to be taken during the fourth week for women who find it easier to remember if they take a pill *every* day.

The phasic pills are an attempt to minimize such side effects as breakthrough bleeding, breast tenderness, etc., by adjusting the hormone levels in the pills to more naturally mimic the woman's normal hormonal cycle. **Bi-phasic pills,** for example, contain one ratio of estrogen to progesterone in pills for the first phase of the cycle (say, the first 7 days) and another ratio of estrogen to progesterone in pills for the second phase of the cycle (say, days 8 through 21). **Tri-phasic pills** seek to fine-tune the hormone balances even further by having differing ratios of estrogens and progesterones for *three* different phases of the cycle.

Mini-pills, on the other hand, contain no estrogen at all—thus avoiding any possible estrogen-related side effects—and work on the basis of progesterone dosage alone. These pills are taken one a day *every* day, with no break from one cycle to the next. We will discuss the mini-pill in more detail in the next chapter.

Which pill is the best? Different doctors (and different users) favor different pills, but a recent study done by the

World Health Organization, comparing all different kinds, found no basic differences between any of them. More important than which kind of pill is used is the matter of *how* the Pill is used and what, if any, side effects the individual user may find between one kind and another.

USING THE PILL

Almost all major brands of the Pill dispensed in the United States today come in "one-cycle packets" for use either with a 21-day cycle of medicine or a 28-day cycle. Whichever your doctor or clinic prescribes, bear in mind that the Pill in any form will only be effective if it is taken *regularly*.

Unfortunately, this doesn't always happen. Occasionally even the most responsible person will accidentally forget to take a pill. And even when the Pill is taken, something may happen to keep it from being absorbed properly. This can happen either because the Pill interacts with some other medicine you are taking or because of some gastrointestinal upset such as vomiting or diarrhea. On page 90, we'll talk about what to do if you forget to take a pill at the right time and point out a list of medicines that can interfere with absorption of the Pill.

When to start. The doctor who prescribes the Pill for you may have strong feelings about this, based on experience with other patients. If so, follow her or his instructions. Most doctors, however, think that starting the Pill on the first day of a menstrual period is the easiest. Years ago doctors thought that the Pill might not be effective in blocking ovulation that first month and advised other contraceptive measures to be used simultaneously until the second cycle. But experience doesn't bear that out—most doctors today believe the Pill is effective immediately as you begin using it, providing instant contraception. Don't be alarmed if you have somewhat more bleeding or spotting during the first month or two after starting the Pill, or some bleeding or spotting in the middle of a cycle. This happens frequently and doesn't mean anything bad; in most cases it stops after the first cycle or two on the Pill.

Once you have started using the Pill on either a 21-day-and-the-skip-7-days basis or on a 28-day regimen with the last 7 pills being blanks, it is important to continue using the Pill on the same cyclic basis without a break. The birth control effect will continue as long as you do so. But if you allow a gap to occur between completion of one cycle of medication and starting the next, you will risk losing the birth control effect. Regularity is the key to success.

What if you decide you want to get pregnant? The effect of the Pill is entirely reversible; when you stop taking it, you will presently begin ovulating again, so that fertilization and pregnancy become possible again. *This may not happen immediately*, however. Although some women who stop taking the Pill become pregnant the very next ovulation cycle, others may require three or four cycles for ovulation to be reestablished, and some women may require even longer. In one recent report in the *Journal of the American Medical Association*, researchers concluded that a period of as long as 13 to 15 months before ovulation recurs is still within normal range. So patience is in order.

What if you forget? When you accidentally forget to take a pill, the chain of hormone-controlled events suppressing ovulation is broken, and ovulation *may* occur, depending on how long the break in the chain happens to be, and what is done about it. *Any* lapse in the regular dosage of pills *may* result in ovulation, and the Pill user has to realize this. A forgotten pill is lost forever. However, there are some rules of thumb to follow any time a pill is forgotten (or vomited up, or passed on out of the intestine due to diarrhea) to help make up for the loss and minimize the chances of contraceptive failure.

If *one* pill is forgotten and you realize the mistake

before the next pill is due, the best thing to do is take the missed pill as soon as you discover the lapse, and then take the next one at the usual time. This is the most common error, and if it doesn't happen too often, it should not usually lead to pregnancy or any other problems.

If the lapse is between 24 and 36 hours, you have missed *two* pills end-running. In this event, according to instructions of the Pill manufacturers, you should take the two missing pills together, and also use *some other form of contraception along with the Pill for the rest of the packet—* a diaphragm or condom, for example. In other words, with such a long lapse, there is a real chance that ovulation may take place and the Pill alone may fail during that cycle. In fact, most doctors feel that the additional form of contraception should be continued for a full 14 days even if you use up the packet of pills you are using and start another. This additional protection should make up for the lapse satisfactorily—unless the lapse has been long enough (like a week or two) for ovulation to have taken place and fertilization to have already occurred. However, a woman using the Pill for birth control should realize from the start that *any* lapse in use can mean potential failure of this birth control method, and the more frequent or more prolonged the lapses, the more risk of unwanted pregnancy. If you find, in practice, that you are a person who just frequently forgets to take medications, or can't remember whether you've taken them or not, you may be a person for whom this form of birth control just isn't suited and should consider some alternative form of birth control that fits in better with your individual life-style.

Drug interactions are an even more dangerous and insidious consideration. A number of other drugs you may be taking, or have to take at one time or another, may interact with the Pill and reduce its effectiveness for preventing ovulation, and this effect could sneak up on you without your knowing it, even if you are taking the Pill with absolute regularity. Such common antibiotics as ampicillin, tetracycline, or rifampin may interact with the Pill, and you should "cover yourself" with additional birth control protection while using them. In addition, sleeping pills containing barbiturates, certain drugs used for treating epilepsy, or certain drugs used to treat arthritis may have similar interactions. You can't be expected to know which drugs might cause interactions and which not, but your doctor can. As a rule of thumb, if a doctor prescribes *any* other medicine while you are taking the Pill, you should remind him or her that you are taking the Pill and *ask* about any possible interaction.

ADVANTAGES OF THE PILL

As we have already seen, the advantages of the Pill are so numerous and so great that for a great many women it is quite simply the best possible form of birth control available. It is easy to use, convenient, and extremely reliable. It can be used with confidence month after month and year after year with virtually no side effects in most cases. Besides providing almost complete freedom from fear of pregnancy, its use is not directly related or connected with sexual intercourse itself, so there is no interference with sexual enjoyment or spontaniety. Women who rely upon it may wish to use some other form of birth control for the first month on the Pill, as an extra safeguard, and may choose to use some other method for a brief period of time after childbirth, but otherwise it can be used continuously. And it is reversible any time the woman desires a pregnancy, simply by dropping off it for a few months. It may take a while to become pregnant, but all evidence indicates that a woman who is fertile before taking the pill will be just as fertile after stopping it to have a baby.

Persons taking the Pill should have a physical examination by a doctor before starting, and the Pill must be prescribed, but otherwise no other examinations are necessary other than the regular periodic health checkup that a person would ordinarily want to have anyway.

The Pill is particularly advantageous for certain special groups of people. It is especially to be recommended for young women who are first becoming sexually active during their teen years, not only because of the excellent protection against unwanted pregnancy but because use of the Pill often straightens out early menstrual problems such as irregular periods or menstrual cramping, so common to young girls, and also provides protection against some forms of sexually transmitted diseases, as we will see below. It is the birth control method of choice for most young women who absolutely *do not want* an accidental pregnancy or for whom such a pregnancy would be a disaster but who want to preserve and protect their ability to have children later.

Interestingly enough, the Pill has been found to confer a number of other health benefits aside from its contraceptive function. Because the Pill hormones maintain the mucus plug in the cervix firm and intact, without cyclic softening, it provides some protection against ascending bacterial infections in the uterus or Fallopian tubes, especially such infections as gonorrhea. Regular Pill users have only about one-half the frequency of such infections as occur in women not taking the Pill. In many women painful periods stop, headaches improve, premenstrual tension symptoms decline, such adolescent plagues as acne improve, and benign (noncancerous) breast lumps are much less common while taking the Pill.

As for cancer, it is now known that the pill also *protects* against both cancer of the ovary and cancer of the inner lining of the uterus—these cancers appear only about half as often in Pill users as in women who have never used the Pill. There is also a lower incidence of cancer of the cervix among Pill users. This may not be so much due to effects of the Pill itself as due to the fact that Pill users are more likely than other women to have more or less regular examinations, including the Pap smears that are so helpful in detecting cancer of the cervix in its very earliest, completely curable stages.

SIDE EFFECTS AND
DISADVANTAGES OF THE PILL

Earlier we mentioned some of the more common minor side effects some women have when taking the Pill. These may include breakthrough bleeding, occasional nausea, breast enlargement or tenderness, increased vaginal mucus discharge, headaches, or water retention leading to weight gain and a feeling of bloatedness. None of these side effects are dangerous, and all may be exaggerated during the first few cycles of Pill use and disappear later. They also tend to be reduced or relieved altogether, in most women, by using a lower dosage pill. Occasionally, however, a woman may be bothered by one or another such side effect so severely or persistently that a different method of contraception must be chosen and the Pill terminated.

Major and important side effects can also occur, although their occurrence is rare. The most important of these is the Pill's possible effects on blood vessels, with an increased risk of blood clots, strokes, or heart attacks. These effects are more frequent and threatening in women over the age of thirty-five, particularly if they are heavy cigarette smokers. With younger, nonsmoking women using low-dose pills, they rarely occur except when the woman is already at risk for this kind of disease (see page 95 for discussion of women who should *not* use the Pill). Among other major —but extremely rare—side effects are the development of benign liver tumors, development of jaundice, or worsening of migraine headaches. In the event of any of these problems, the Pill user should consult her doctor and, very possibly, discontinue pill use.

What about fears that the Pill may cause cancer? All evidence today indicates that this possible side effect just doesn't exist. There is no conclusive evidence that the Pill can cause or contribute to the development of any kind of cancer at all. If there were any long-term trends toward cancer among Pill users *as a result of the Pill,* those trends would have shown up by now, and they haven't. In particular, no connection has been found between the Pill and breast cancer—one of the cancers known to be affected by hormonal influences in the woman's body, and therefore the most suspect. In the mid-1980s several studies involving thousands of women using the Pill demonstrated no increased incidence of breast cancer no matter how long the women had used the Pill or how early in life they had started. And, in 1986, a study reported by the Centers for Disease Control in Atlanta indicated that this no-cancer link applied even to women who had strong family histories of breast cancer. In fact, as we mentioned above, there is evidence that long-term use of the Pill may actually *protect* against certain kinds of cancer, as well as several other serious female conditions (See *"Advantages of the Pill,"* above).

Since major complications of the Pill *can* occur in some women, this means that the Pill may not be the best answer for everybody. The most worrisome and dangerous side effects—the problems of blood clotting and the possible development of heart attacks or strokes—are known to increase in older women or in those with special risk factors. Most authorities today therefore recommend that women in the following groups should *not* use the Pill because of increased risks of side effects:

1) Women over the age of thirty-five should not start the Pill or, if already using it, should discontinue it in favor of some other form of birth control. This is doubly true if the woman is a heavy cigarette smoker (defined as ten to fifteen cigarettes a day). Both age and cigarette smoking are separate risk factors for blood clotting troubles, and the two risk factors together compound each other.

2) Even *younger* women who are heavy cigarette

smokers should choose another form of birth control because of the increased risk of blood clotting problems with the Pill. The increased risk on this account disappears almost immediately and completely, however, if the woman stops smoking.

3) Any woman who *already has* blood clotting problems, high blood pressure, coronary artery disease or other forms of heart disease, or a history of strokes or other cerebral vascular problems should avoid the Pill and probably should never take it. One reason for a medical examination before starting the Pill is to help identify women with these risk factors and turn them away from the Pill as a birth control method.

4) Any women with close relatives who have had heart attacks or other severe disease of the heart or blood vessels, especially at an early age (i.e., in their thirties) should probably not use the Pill or at least should seek a specialist's advice before starting it. This is especially true if the woman is also a smoker.

5) Women with other illnesses, especially diabetes, kidney, or liver disease, should seek special advice before starting the Pill. Having such illnesses does not necessarily mean that a woman can't use the Pill, especially in low-dose forms, but closer-than-normal doctor's supervision may be necessary to avoid problems.

6) Finally, any woman who *already* has a breast cancer, cancer of the cervix, or any other cancer that might be affected by increased doses of hormones is not suited to using the Pill and should choose some alternative form of birth control.

There is one resource that every user of the Pill should avail herself of—the manufacturer's package insert placed in every package of pills sold in this country. This piece of literature reviews in detail how the Pill works, how it should be taken, what side effects to watch out for, and other things a Pill user should know. Read it when you first start using the Pill, and review it once a year or so; then check *any-*

thing you don't understand with the prescribing doctor. A large proportion of unexpected pregnancies among Pill users occur simply because the woman misunderstands how the Pill is to be used or fails to understand what to do when something seemingly unexpected happens.

EFFECTIVENESS OF THE PILL

Many studies of thousands of women using the Pill regularly and correctly have concluded that under ideal circumstances it will be more than 99 percent effective in preventing pregnancy. Any couple understanding this method of birth control and using it with unfailing regularity, or using alternative methods during any possible lapses, can expect that degree of effectiveness. Overall, the Pill has proven more effective than any other form of birth control known, short of sterilization.

OTHER HORMONE CONTRACEPTIVES

Useful as the combined-hormone pill may be for many women as a birth control method, there are some who can't —or shouldn't—use it. Yet using hormone medications to control or prevent pregnancies obviously has some striking advantages over other birth control methods. As soon as it became clear that many of the problems and disadvantages connected with the combined-hormone pill were largely related to the estrogens those pills contained, researchers began to explore an equally effective hormone birth control pill that didn't contain any estrogen at all. The result was the development of the progesterone-only pill, the so-called mini-pill. For many women this has proved to be a very satisfactory alternative to the estrogen-containing pill, although the mini-pill has some problems of its own.

In addition, certain different *forms* of hormone-based birth control methods were studied and are now available —or soon will be. On the forefront of research today, for example, are the long-acting implantable or injectable hormone birth control preparations. These involve placing a deposit of hormone somewhere in the body in a way that the hormone dissolves very slowly, making a little bit available each day without the woman having to think about taking pills or anything else, as long as the implanted medication lasts. Several forms have been developed and are in use in other parts of the world; in the United States such preparations are still considered "experimental" or "investigational" and do not yet have the approval of the Food and Drug Administration for general use. But sooner or later some such preparations will be approved and may well meet the needs of many women.

Finally, the development of hormone-based contraceptives has made another *kind* of birth control method available: the so-called morning-after pill. One of the major problems with *any* birth control method is that people occasionally fail to use it, or some accident or happenstance renders it useless—a condom that breaks or slips off in the midst of use, for example. In general, the idea of "morning after" birth control has acquired an unsavory reputation, probably based on a narrow moralistic attitude that people aren't *supposed* to make mistakes or have accidents with birth control, and that, if they do, they deserve the consequences. But after all, the whole idea of birth control is to prevent unwanted pregnancies, and unfortunately, people are not perfect. "Morning after" birth control is certainly not a neat, orderly, or desirable approach to birth control under ordinary circumstances, nor is it readily available, on demand, for anyone who wants it. It can cause serious nausea or vomiting, and many clinics and doctors are reluctant to prescribe it. But it should be mentioned, at least, as a possible recourse when a woman is exposed to unwanted pregnancy as a result of rape or assault, for example.

THE "MINI-PILL"

The popular name "mini-pill" is unfortunate because it doesn't really mean what it says. This is not some miniaturized or tailored-down version of the combined-hormone pill, nor does it contain any kind of mini-dose of its active hormone. It is simply a hormone-type contraceptive pill which contains only one of the two female hormones found in the combined pill—a synthetic progesterone-like hormone with no estrogen at all. Therefore, it is more accurate to speak of it as a *progesterone-only* pill.

One of the first clues that hormone medications could be used for birth control purposes came in the 1940s when researchers discovered that high doses of progesterone alone would prevent rabbits from getting pregnant. But even today, strange to say, nobody knows for sure exactly *how or why* the progesterone-only pill works.

One thing is certain: it doesn't work exactly like the combined estrogen-progesterone pill. With the combined pill, the combination of estrogen and progesterone completely block ovulation so that a ripened ovum cannot be formed. With the progesterone-only pill, this doesn't necessarily happen—it only seems to block ovulation in some women some of the time. This pill depends on other progesterone actions for its effectiveness. For one thing, it causes the mucus plug in the cervical canal to remain thick and dense, so sperm have great difficulty penetrating into the uterus. In addition, the progesterone creates a "hostile environment" in the uterus, so that even if sperm do penetrate and fertilize an ovum, that fertilized ovum is unable to embed itself in the uterine lining and grow into a pregnancy. Whatever the combination of effects, the progesterone-only pill has proven very effective at preventing pregnancies. Although not *quite* as effective as the combination pill, the "mini-pill" comes close, with only 2 to 3 pregnancies per 100 women per year, or 97-98 percent effectiveness.

How the mini-pill is used. Like the combined pill, the progesterone-only pill is taken regularly once a day, beginning on the first day of a regular menstrual period. But unlike the combined pill, the progesterone-only pill should then be taken regularly once a day, *every day of the year—*

there is no break in pill-taking, no 21-days-on, 7-days-off cycle. You continue taking a pill every day, right on through your next period of menstrual bleeding, and the next, and the next, without a break. It's smart to get in the habit of taking the mini-pill at the same time every day, preferably at bedtime, and you must *continue daily, without interruption, whether bleeding occurs or not.*

A great many women find that their pattern of bleeding changes significantly, especially during the first few months after starting on the mini-pill. For most women, bleeding becomes more scanty and irregular, with no particular relation to former normal menstrual periods, and with frequent bleeding or spotting in between periods. Others may have irregular or unpredictable intervals of more heavy or prolonged bleeding, while some may develop longer-than-usual gaps between their menstrual periods. Within reasonable limits, such changes are normal with this medication, or at least to be expected. They don't mean that the Pill isn't working—in fact, they provide good evidence that the Pill *is* working. Two extremes of menstrual irregularity on the Pill, however, require medical attention. If you have repeated or prolonged heavy bleeding, for example, you should consult with your doctor, who may find that you should discontinue the mini-pill and depend on some other form of birth control. Similarly, if you are one of the few who have no bleeding at all for as long as 45 days, it could mean that there has been a failure of contraception and that you may be pregnant. In such a case, stop taking the Pill immediately, substitute another form of contraception (a diaphragm or condom, for example) and consult your doctor, who will determine whether you are pregnant or not before instructing you to resume the Pill.

What if you should happen to forget and miss taking one or more pills? As with any birth control method, this one only works if you use it. If you forget to take a pill at the regular time, there is a chance, however small, that you may become pregnant, and that chance of becoming pregnant increases with every successive pill you miss. Here is the procedure to follow, as outlined by one progesterone-only pill manufacturer: If you have missed taking one pill, take it as soon as you remember it, and also take the next pill at the regular time—which will mean you will have taken two pills within one 24-hour period. (This is fine, and shouldn't cause any trouble.) If you have missed two pills in a row, take one of the missed pills as soon as you remember it, discard the second missed pill, and then take your regular pill for that day at the regular time. But, in addition, because you may have ovulated during the missed-pill days and would in that case be unprotected, you should use an additional form of birth control *along with* taking the mini-pill until you have a menstrual period, or until your doctor determines that you aren't pregnant. All this means, of course, that you should be consulting your doctor immediately if you have missed two or more pills in a row, or if you don't have a menstrual period for 45 days since the last one.

Incidentally, all this isn't as complicated as it may seem, once you have started this medicine, and it is all explained in clear detail in the printed leaflet that comes with every package of mini-pills. Anyone using the progesterone-only pill, just like anyone using the combined pill, should *read the package insert* before starting the medicine, check with the doctor about anything that isn't clear, and then review the package insert periodically, not only to refresh your memory, but because sometimes important new information may have been added.

Advantages of the mini-pill. The major advantage of the progesterone-only pill is that it doesn't contain any estrogen. Since many of the serious possible complications of the combination pill—such problems as blood clots, strokes, heart attacks, etc.—are believed to be caused by the estrogen component, the progesterone-only pill should be relatively free of these side effects, at least in theory, and therefore safer to use than the combined pill. Unfortunately, this theoretical "greater safety" factor has not yet been thoroughly confirmed by careful, large-volume scientific studies, so it still has to be considered theory, not established fact. But because so many of the potential complications of the combination pill appear more likely to occur in older women who have used the Pill for a long time than in younger women, it may well prove to be wise for a woman who has been using the combined pill during younger years to switch to the progesterone-only pill after the age of 30 or 35 as an extra precaution. Similarly, the progesterone-only pill may be a better choice than the combined pill for women who are heavy cigarette smokers, or who have family histories of heart disease or high blood pressure, but still are willing to accept the risk of using some kind of hormone contraceptive because of its high effectiveness and simplicity of use.

Disadvantages of the mini-pill. The main disadvantage of the progesterone-only pill is the frequency of irregular bleeding problems. For some women the problem is fairly minor, the sort of thing they can easily put up with, just a matter of bleeding or spotting at odd times between periods, and having rather scanty, or else heavier-than-normal periods when the flow starts. But obviously, if a woman is having such frequent bleeding and spotting at unpredictable intervals that it is interfering with her sex life, or if she is missing periods completely so often that she is constantly wondering if she is pregnant or not, this form of contraception could become more of a burden than a help. Fortunately, these irregular bleeding patterns, in most women using the mini-pill, do seem to settle down into more regular, predictable patterns after a few months of use. (Maybe this seems to be true simply because the women in whom the problem *doesn't* settle down don't continue using the mini-pill very long, so that the ones using it for longer periods are automatically the ones who don't have such severe problems.)

What if you become pregnant while taking the progesterone-only pill? Many studies have indicated that a woman who has an accidental pregnancy while taking *any* of the hormone contraceptives has as much risk as any other woman of an abnormal pregnancy, plus a slight additional risk of fetal heart or limb abnormalities due to the possible effects of the hormones themselves on the fetus. This holds true of an accidental pregnancy while taking the progesterone-only pill—a slightly increased risk that the baby might have a heart defect or a limb-reduction defect. But with the mini-pill, some medical authorities suspect there may be an additional risk: that the pregnancy may be **ectopic**—that is, be located in a Fallopian tube rather than normally situated in the uterus, an extremely dangerous kind of pregnancy which terminates very early, often with severe hemorrhage. This may be true because the progesterone slows down muscular movement in the tube, which normally carries the fertilized egg down to the uterus. This suspicion has not yet, in fact, been proven, and greater experience with the mini-pill may presently show that this is an unfounded worry—but for now, it is one possibility that needs to be considered.

If the mini-pill *is* almost as effective as the combined pill, and if it *may* be safer than the combined pill in terms of threatening side effects, and if most women find that the irregular bleeding problems settle down after the first few months of mini-pill use, then why isn't the mini-pill used more widely than it is? Probably the answer is that everybody likes to go with a winner, and the combined pill, which was developed and marketed first, has proved to be a winner for many women, who therefore want to stick with it, and women who are just starting birth control tend to follow their older sisters. The real importance of the mini-pill is that it provides an alternative choice with almost the same effectiveness as the combination pill for any woman who for any reason wants to change.

LONG-ACTING
HORMONE CONTRACEPTIVES

Although "pill" type oral contraceptives, whether combined or progesterone-only, are suitable for a great many women in a great many situations, they have their limits. Estrogen pills carry the risk of potential side effects. Progesterone-only mini-pills can cause troublesome irregular bleeding. And *all* oral contraceptives involve the inconvenience of having to take medicine on a regular daily schedule. Many women object to this—and indeed, failures of these contraceptives can most often be traced to women failing to take the pills on the rigid schedule necessary. This is trouble enough in modern Western countries where medicines are readily available at any drugstore and people are accustomed to taking pills; the problem is much aggravated in less developed countries where pill-taking is not the cultural norm and where medicines are not available just down the street. And, indeed, numerous studies have shown that oral contraceptives are, in practice, far less effective, with much higher failure rates, in underdeveloped countries, for example, than in the United States or Europe The problem isn't with the Pill; it's with the user.

Because of these considerations, a great deal of effort and research has gone into the development of long-acting hormone contraceptives—contraceptives that require only one dose of medicine every three months, or six months, or a year or so, and then remain fully effective until time for the next dose. So far, most of these efforts have been focused on progesterone-only preparations and are either still considered experimental or "investigational" in this country, and are not yet approved by the Food and Drug Administration for general use—but they may represent the wave of the future.

Long-acting progestogens. Two long-acting progestogen preparations have been explored and studied. Both depend on exactly the same principle as the progesterone-only mini-pill except that the drug, instead of being taken in daily doses by mouth, is placed in a long-acting preparation which, when injected into the body, dissolves very slowly, releasing just a small amount of the progesterone every day automatically until all the medicine in the dose is gone. In one such preparation, known as Depo-Provera, the progestogen is in the form of micro-crystals of different sizes suspended in a watery saline solution; once injected, the crystals dissolve and the progestogen is slowly absorbed. This is a case of an older drug being put to a new use. Depo-Provera was first developed more than twenty years ago—and still is used in large doses—for treating uterine cancer. Later it was tried unsuccessfully as a medicine to prevent miscarriages and premature labor. Finally, in the early 1960s, it was tested as a long-acting contraceptive. Once injected, the drug remained active in the body for a period of about three months. In a second preparation, known as Noristerat, the progestogen is injected in an oily or waxy base and is then slowly released into the bloodstream, with a single dose lasting about 60 days. Both these preparations not only acted on cervical mucus and the uterine lining to prevent pregnancy, but actually blocked ovulation in most cases.

Such preparations have the obvious advantage that they are easier to administer than daily tablets, and, once injected, women don't have to worry about forgetting to take pills. Both disturb normal menstrual patterns just the same as the mini-pill does. Most women experienced irregular periods with spotting in between; some had very heavy bleeding, while others stopped menstrual bleeding completely, raising the question of pregnancy. But the main worry about these drugs was the question of whether they might not, over long use, contribute to the development of breast or uterine cancer. Most studies have indicated that no such link with cancer exists with these preparations, but while they have been approved for use in England and much of Europe, in the United States they are still considered "investigational" and do not at present have FDA approval for general use as contraceptives.

Progesterone implants. Other newer long-acting progesterone preparations are also now beginning to appear. All these preparations involve enclosing a progestogen medication in some kind of container which can be implanted in the body and then allow small amounts of the hormone to seep out into the bloodstream each day. In one case, the hormone is enclosed in small silicone-plastic cylinders which can be buried under the skin. Other preparations enclose the hormone in small pellets with dissolvable coatings; the pellets with thin coatings dissolve first, those with thicker coatings dissolve later. In still another method, the hormone is enclosed in the hollow core of a silicone-plastic vaginal ring which can be inserted in the vagina. These rings contain enough hormone to last for about six months; the woman can then remove the ring herself and insert a new one—or she can remove the ring any time she wants to reestablish normal menstrual periods or become pregnant. Some implantable-cylinder-type preparations could, in theory, remain active for five years or more. They have the disadvantage that they require a minor surgical operation to implant them (under the skin of the arm, for example)—but have the advantage that they can be removed at any time if the woman decides for any reason she doesn't like this long-term form of contraception.

Such implantable contraceptives have been tried out in various parts of the world, most notably in Sweden, but are still considered experimental in the United States. If ongoing patient trials show that these preparations really do work well for prolonged periods of time, provide reliable and effective birth control, and have no more side effects than other hormone contraceptives, they will surely become available for general use sooner or later. And they will provide an alternative form of birth control that many women could find more convenient and suitable than any other method.

MORNING-AFTER CONTRACEPTION

Occasionally, known failures of birth control efforts occur: a condom breaks during intercourse, a diaphragm is forgotten, sex relations occur unexpectedly in the absence of any protection, a woman is raped and faces the possibility of an unacceptable pregnancy—the reasons are legion. Fortunately, there are several measures that can be taken "the morning after" to ensure that a possible pregnancy does not develop.

One measure is the immediate insertion of an intrauterine device, or IUD. (See chapter eight for details about IUDs.) This device, placed in the uterus, will prevent the implantation of a fertilized egg, if fertilization occurred, so a pregnancy will not ensue. If left in place, the device will also prevent the need for morning-after birth control in the future because it is in itself an effective continuing birth control device.

There are also ways that the combination pill or the progesterone-only pill can be prescribed for morning-after birth control. Because serious nausea, vomiting, and other side effects frequently occur, most clinics are reluctant to prescribe these methods, which have to be authorized by a doctor.

Finally, an experimental medication known as RU 486 has recently been tested in Europe as a morning-after birth control method. This drug brings about very early miscarriage or loss of a fertilized ovum. It is not generally available anywhere at this time, and because its effect is, in fact, to induce very early abortion, it may never be generally available in this country.

8

INTRAUTERINE DEVICES (IUDs)

From the early 1960s until the mid-1980s yet another kind of birth control method has been widely used by women in the United States and other countries—the so-called intra-uterine devices, or IUDs. This form of birth control involves the more or less permanent emplacement, by a doctor, of a small plastic device inside the cavity of a woman's uterus, where it can be left indefinitely to protect against unwanted pregnancies.

The IUD works entirely differently from other birth control methods we have discussed so far. There are no pills to be taken, no sheaths or diaphragms to be placed before intercourse and then removed. Once an IUD is in place, it can just be left there for intervals ranging from one to five years, depending on the particular device. Nor, with most IUDs, is there any disturbance in the woman's normal ovulation and menstrual cycles, no synthetic hormones interfering with her body's normal hormonal balances. When properly placed, the IUD has proven between 97 and 99 percent effective, a reliability record almost as good as for the Pill. It is convenient and hassle-free for most women who use it; and it can be removed any time the woman wants to have a baby, without any effect on her future fertility—at least in most cases. In fact, for a rather large, select group of women, the IUD has been the most totally satisfactory birth control method ever invented.

Unfortunately, the continued availability of IUDs in the United States is very much in question today, at least for the near future, because all but one of the manufacturers of these devices in this country have voluntarily withdrawn them from the market. This has happened, even though IUDs still have full FDA approval, because a few women who have claimed to have been damaged by the use of IUDs have successfully sued the manufacturers and won multimillion-dollar court settlements, thus creating such a liability risk that the manufacturers have simply stopped selling the devices—not for scientific or medical reasons but because of what the companies call "unwarranted litigation and unavailability of liability insurance." However, since IUDs *are* still available in the United States from one manufacturer, at least for the time being, and are still widely available in other countries (including Canada), it is important that we include in this book some basic information about them, how they are used, how they work, and what problems may arise with their use.

WHAT ARE IUDs?

Essentially, an IUD is a small object made of thin plastic which can be rolled up and passed through the cervical canal into the interior cavity of the uterus and then left there more or less indefinitely. (Some IUDs can be left in place for as long as five years if desired.) A couple of nylon threads attached to the lower end of the device are left hanging out of the cervix into the vagina so that the IUD can be removed by a doctor. A doctor must insert the device in the course of a pelvic examination. The IUD is rolled up into a very narrow insertion tube for passage through the cervical canal and the tube is then withdrawn, allowing the device to unroll and remain lodged inside.

IUDs have been made in a variety of shapes and materials. Some open up like little coils or loops. Some are shaped like children's jacks, some like small shields, etc. (See figure 10.) Because an IUD opens out to full size and shape after insertion, it is not ordinarily expelled during menstrual periods. Insertion of the devices is often accompanied by some momentary cramping and discomfort, and most doctors prefer to wait until the woman is in the middle of a menstrual period for insertion. This has two advantages: at such a time it's quite certain that the woman is not already pregnant, and the cervical canal at that time is slightly opened and relaxed so that insertion is easier. In any event, most women have only a little discomfort at the time of insertion, which takes just a couple of minutes. The one IUD still available in the United States is impregnated with progesterone, which is gradually released over a prolonged interval, on the theory that this may enhance its effectiveness.

HOW DOES
AN IUD WORK?

Even the experts are not 100 percent sure of this. The most likely explanation is that the IUD within the uterine cavity acts as a foreign body which the uterine muscle would like to expel but can't. To some degree this foreign body acts as a barrier to sperm finding their way up toward the Fallopian tubes—but even more important, it disturbs the environment inside the uterus so that a fertilized ovum can't become implanted properly or grow. (Of course, a progesterone substance in the IUD would enhance this pregnancy-hostile environment in the uterus.) This means that even when a ripened ovum is released and is fertilized by a sperm, the fertilized cell can't get established in the uterus and develop into a pregnancy.

EXAMPLES OF IUDs

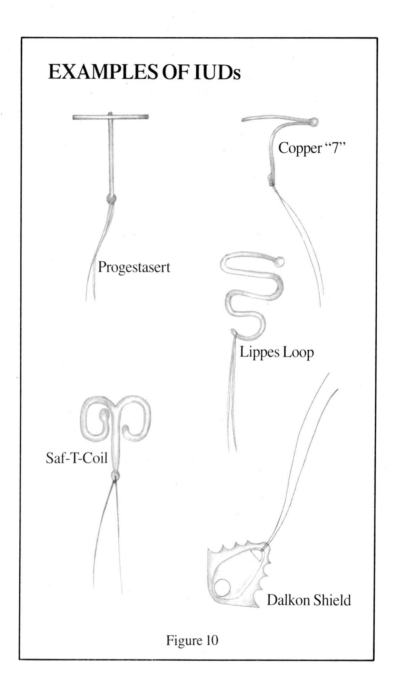

Copper "7"

Progestasert

Lippes Loop

Saf-T-Coil

Dalkon Shield

Figure 10

ADVANTAGES OF THE IUD

The main advantages of the IUD are *convenience* and *reliability*. Once in place the IUD requires virtually no further attention from the user until such time as she wants it removed in order to become pregnant. No barrier needs to be placed before intercourse and then removed afterward. The IUD has no effect on the woman's ovulation cycle nor on the timing of her menstrual periods. There is no alteration, temporary or permanent, in her normal hormonal balances (unless, of course, the IUD is one combined with progesterone). She can proceed with her sexual activity with no further thought about protection against pregnancy. And, in practice, the IUD has proved to be one of the most reliable forms of birth control, with only about 1 to 3 pregnancies per 100 women per year. The IUD is especially suitable for many older women who have already had all the children they want but are reaching an age at which they worry about increased risks from using the Pill, or for older women who have avoided the Pill because they were cigarette smokers. And, for very busy younger women who just don't want to have to remember various pills or devices, the IUD can be a more ideal birth control method than any other.

DISADVANTAGES OF THE IUD

The major disadvantage of the IUD is that many women suffer cramping and discomfort immediately after the IUD is placed. This isn't surprising, since the IUD is a "foreign body" which might be expected to irritate the uterine muscle to some degree just by being there. For most women this problem subsides in a few days or at least after the first period or two, but for some it can remain a recurring problem with each menstrual period. Other women find their menstrual flow increased to a bothersome degree. And for the young woman who has never had a baby, placement of the IUD can be painful; it is far easier to insert in a woman whose cervical canal has been opened and stretched at least once by the delivery of a baby. In addition, there are occasional problems—actually very rare—in which an IUD can be expelled during a menstrual period without the woman knowing it. Even more uncommonly, IUDs have been known to penetrate the uterine wall or even escape into the abdomen. This kind of problem occurs less and less frequently as doctors have developed more experience and skill in placing these devices.

Unfortunately, as more and more women used IUDs and more experience was gathered, two more serious disadvantages appeared. For one thing, women using an IUD seemed more likely to develop **pelvic inflammatory disease** —bacterial infection developing in the uterus or tubes or surrounding tissues. Often these were women who had had pelvic infections such as gonorrhea before starting with an IUD and still harbored organisms in their pelvic organs— but some women developed trouble without any evidence of previous infection. Some of these women suffered so much damage and scarring of their tubes from these infections that they were rendered permanently sterile, and a few women died of the infections. As mentioned earlier, rare cases of this sort led to lawsuits against the manufacturers of IUDs, with people claiming that the IUDs caused the problems; when some companies found themselves faced with multimillion-dollar judgments on account of such problems, even when the problems were exceedingly rare and not necessarily clearly the fault of the IUDs, those companies felt they had no alternative but to discontinue manufacturing or supplying the IUDs.

One other complication also appeared: although pregnancies were extremely rare in women using IUDs, pregnancies occasionally did occur, and when they did, those pregnancies often developed as dangerous ectopic pregnancies—pregnancies that implanted and developed somewhere in the Fallopian tubes instead of the uterus. Since there is not room there for a pregnancy to grow, ectopic pregnancies are almost always lost very early, and in far too many cases the loss can be accompanied by rupture and such severe bleeding as to be life-threatening, requiring emergency surgical treatment.

Overall, experience with IUDs has shown them to be highly convenient and effective, with the risk of trouble very low. Many women have weighed the great benefits against the low risk and elected to use IUDs. But growing medical evidence that the risk of pelvic infection and other complications is actually greater than originally believed, and the legal and economic realities of costly lawsuits, have slowed the use of IUDs in this country. At present only one company offers them for sale in the United States, and many doctors are now refusing to insert them for fear that *they* may be held liable in the event of later untoward problems. Only time will tell whether these attitudes and circumstances will change.

9

STERILIZATION

When we spoke earlier of the "ideal" birth control method, we emphasized that one of its important characteristics would be its *reversibility*—so that when it was discontinued, the woman would quickly regain her capacity to become pregnant. For women who may someday want to become pregnant, reversibility of birth control is a major consideration. And all the birth control methods we have discussed so far have had the features of ready reversibility any time that a pregnancy was desired.

Recent surveys reveal, however, that one of the most popular and widely-used methods of birth control today in the United States is sterilization of either the man or the woman—the one method that is intended to be, and in most cases actually is, *ir*reversible.

Sterilization in either sex involves a surgical procedure to permanently block off the tubes—the vas deferens in the man, the Fallopian tubes in the woman—that carry the male or female sex cells to their intended meeting place, where fertilization of the ripened ovum can take place. You can think of it as the ultimate "barrier method" of birth control. If sperm can't be ejaculated by the man, or if the woman's tubes are blocked so that sperm can't reach a ripened ovum, pregnancy can't take place—at least not as a result of conventional sexual intercourse. For couples who have had all the children they ever want, this may be absolutely the ideal situation, exactly what is wanted for both the present and future.

Unfortunately, one reason for this popularity of sterilization may lie in a widespread—and often tragically incorrect—idea: that sterilization today can be reversed at will. This is simply not the case. True enough, among men and women who have undergone sterilization, a *very small number* have later had the sterilization successfully reversed as a result of an extremely difficult, delicate, and expensive surgical procedure. It *can be done* in some cases—but such procedures are beyond the surgical skill of most surgeons, so that their success rates are very low overall; and, even in the most skillful and experienced hands, there is only about a 50 percent success rate among patients who have been carefully screened and selected to have the best possible chances for success. In a great many cases, the reversal surgery can't even be attempted. Thus, for the vast majority of people, the plain fact is that if sterilization is performed, it is going to be permanent and irreversible.

Sterilization can certainly provide extremely reliable protection against unwanted pregnancy. But no one should consider a sterilization procedure with the idea that it is some kind of temporary measure that can easily be reversed sometime in the future.

MALE STERILIZATION
(VASECTOMY)

A vasectomy—the surgical removal of a short segment of the man's sperm tube on each side—is a basically simple surgical procedure. It is usually done under a local anesthetic right in the doctor's office or clinic and takes about fifteen minutes. After the anesthetic injection, the surgeon makes a small incision in the scrotum, ties off each of the two sperm-carrying tubes, removes a three-quarter-inch segment of each tube, and then returns the tubes to the scrotum and closes the skin incision with a stitch or two. Thus each tube is completely interrupted, with firm ties on the cut ends above and below the interruption. (See figure 11.) Ordinarily the patient can go on home a few minutes after the procedure is over. The surgeon will advise him to wear brief-type undershorts or an athletic supporter (jockstrap) for several days and to take a couple of warm tub baths a day to keep the incision clean and aid healing. On rare occasions there may be a little bleeding at the site of the operation or even the formation of a small blood clot, or **hematoma,** but even this will heal quickly with the aid of the warm baths. On *very* rare occasions a patient may develop a small lump called a **sperm granuloma** where the tube has been cut; this causes no trouble unless it becomes bulky or painful, in which case it can be removed later. Aside from these minor and uncommon problems, the procedure is uncomplicated.

Sterility is not immediate after a vasectomy because there are already large numbers of sperm "downstream" from the tied tubes, stored in the upper vas or in the seminal vesicles. These sperm remain very active, and it may take weeks for them all to be evacuated by ejaculation. In most clinics the patient will be asked to bring in a semen specimen collected in a condom or obtained by masturbation three months after the vasectomy, and another specimen a month later. If both those specimens are completely free of sperm, the vasectomy is considered successful and the man can expect to be sterile thereafter. Of course, he should use some other form of birth control during this "waiting period."

Occasionally, a vasectomy doesn't work. There is always a possibility, however unlikely, that the ties may work off and the cut ends of a vas may find each other and heal

ROUTE OF THE SPERM

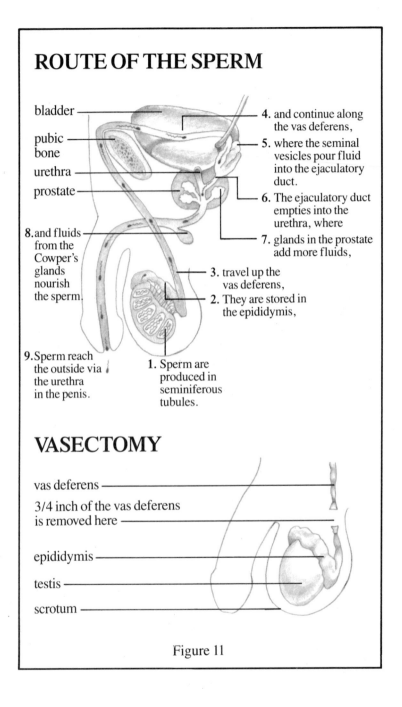

bladder

pubic bone

urethra

prostate

8. and fluids from the Cowper's glands nourish the sperm.

9. Sperm reach the outside via the urethra in the penis.

4. and continue along the vas deferens,

5. where the seminal vesicles pour fluid into the ejaculatory duct.

6. The ejaculatory duct empties into the urethra, where

7. glands in the prostate add more fluids,

3. travel up the vas deferens,

2. They are stored in the epididymis,

1. Sperm are produced in seminiferous tubules.

VASECTOMY

vas deferens

3/4 inch of the vas deferens is removed here

epididymis

testis

scrotum

Figure 11

back together. There is even an occasional man who has a third (or even a fourth!) vas deferens that the surgeon didn't find and didn't suspect was there. But these are extremely rare occurrences, and in either case, the three-month and four-month semen specimens would still show sperm present. In such a case the vasectomy would be considered a failure, and usually the surgeon would explore the area under a general anesthetic to determine what the problem was and correct it.

In the vast majority of cases, however, the sperm tests are negative, and the man thereafter will never ejaculate any sperm. His testicles will continue to manufacture sperm, but these cells will simply be harmlessly absorbed by the body. Indeed, in some men, after a period of time, the immune system will begin to regard these sperm as "foreign" cells and start making antibodies to help destroy them. As we will see, this can be a problem in the event that a reversal of the vasectomy is attempted later.

What about effects on the man's health after a vasectomy? This question has been carefully investigated, and vasectomy seems to have no worrisome physical effects of any sort, either immediately after the operation or years later. There is no alteration in the man's biochemistry or his hormone balances and no evidence of any long-term physical illnesses related to vasectomy. Male erections occur as usual, orgasm and ejaculation (without sperm) occur as usual, and there is no diminishment of sexual pleasure, staying power, or anything else. But doctors aren't quite so sure about *emotional* effects of vasectomy. In general, there don't seem to be any widespread, characteristic patterns of emotional distress in vasectomized men—yet psychiatrists tell us that some men do have emotionally related problems or disturbances in sexual function. Some, for example, may come to think of themselves as castrated or having lost their manhood following vasectomy. Others may have difficulty coping with the idea that they can't make their wives pregnant any longer but that somebody else could or may feel that women no longer regard them as virile males. There is no way to predict such emotional reactions in advance, but it probably would make sense for a man who already has some problem with his sexual function, or who is involved in an unstable or disintegrating sexual relationship, to postpone vasectomy until such problems have been thoroughly resolved. A vasectomy is unlikely to help *cure* any such problem, and it may well, in some cases, make it worse.

FEMALE STERILIZATION
(TUBAL LIGATION OR TL)

Sterilization in the female involves exactly the same idea as in the male, except that it is the Fallopian tubes between the ovaries and the uterus that are tied and cut to prevent a ripened ovum from meeting an active sperm. The main difference is a problem in logistics: it is a more difficult procedure to do successfully in a woman than in a man.

The principle and the operation itself are much the same. The surgeon must first find and identify the Fallopian tube on either side. A silk tie or ligature is tied around each tube, a segment of tube is cut out or otherwise destroyed, and the other loose end of each tube then tied off, so that each tube has two tied ends and a gap in between. (See figure 12.) A variety of methods may be used to make sure that a portion of each tube is destroyed. In some cases a segment of tube may be removed surgically on each side; in other cases a segment on each side may be destroyed by an **electrocautery.** Some surgeons take special precautions that the cut ends of the tubes not find each other and rejoin: one cut end, for instance, may be buried in the muscular wall of the uterus, or the cut and tied ends may be doubled back on themselves and tied again. (Sometimes clips are used instead of ties.) Of course, any such surgical manipulation is later followed by scarring, which further permanently seals the ends of the tubes apart. The problem is that the more of the tube is cut out or destroyed, or is later in-

TUBAL LIGATION
Figure 12

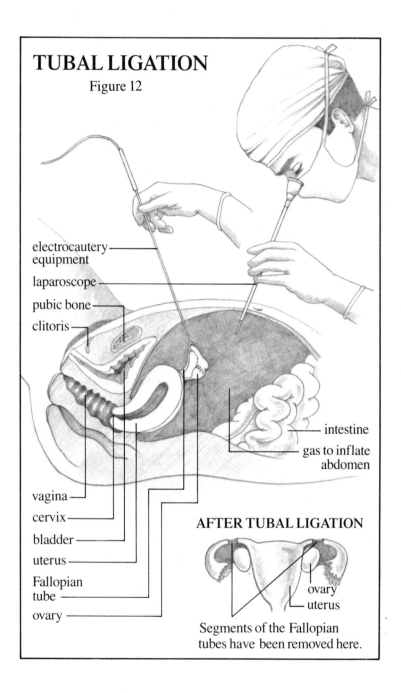

electrocautery equipment

laparoscope

pubic bone

clitoris

intestine

gas to inflate abdomen

vagina

cervix

bladder

uterus

Fallopian tube

ovary

AFTER TUBAL LIGATION

ovary

uterus

Segments of the Fallopian tubes have been removed here.

volved in scarring during healing, thus making the sterilization more reliable, the more difficult—or even impossible
—it may be later to repair and rejoin those tubes in the
event that a reversal is attempted.

How long the **tubal ligation** procedure takes, and how
hard it is on the woman, depends on how it is done. A few
years ago it required a so-called **abdominal laparotomy,** or
"exploratory" incision in the abdomen, done under a general anesthesia, with two or three days in the hospital necessary for recovery. Today the procedure is more likely to be
done more simply by methods known as **laparoscopy** or
culdoscopy. With laparoscopy, a tiny incision is made in the
abdominal wall and a narrow, lighted observation tube is
inserted. The Fallopian tubes are located and visualized
through this instrument; then a second instrument for cutting and tying, or for cautery and tying, is inserted through
a second tiny incision, so that the operation is done under
direct visualization without having to make a large abdominal incision. This procedure usually takes only twenty
minutes or so, under local anesthesia, and the woman may
be allowed to go home that evening or the following morning. With culdoscopy, the incision is made through the
upper end of the vagina and a similar direct-vision procedure done, without requiring any abdominal incision at all.
The procedure by culdoscopy is very commonly used today
in other parts of the world, but laparoscopy is the method
of choice in the United States.

After a tubal ligation there is no particular "waiting
period" because sterilization is accomplished the moment
the procedure is completed. There are certain possible problems, however, that a woman should know about. A TL
does involve surgical manipulation inside the abdomen, so
the woman is likely to have a few days of abdominal pain
or discomfort following the procedure, however it is done.
The procedure is significantly more expensive than a vasectomy, with hospital costs in addition to the surgeon's fee,
and some health insurance plans may not pay for steriliza-

tion procedures. What is more, occasionally a tubal ligation will fail and a woman will become pregnant in spite of it. There have been cases in which the ties came off the tubes and the cut ends found each other and healed back together —uncommon, but not impossible. It is also a more difficult procedure, technically, for the surgeon, who might occasionally misidentify a tube and, for example, cut and tie one of the supporting ligaments of the uterus by mistake instead of the Fallopian tube. (Of course, pathological examination of a removed segment would identify this error, so that the procedure could quickly be repeated—but if the "tube" is cauterized, nothing is removed for the pathologist to examine, and the first news that there was an error might be an unexpected pregnancy.)

There is one other problem to consider: when there *is* a failure and a pregnancy occurs, there is an increased risk that it will be a dangerous ectopic or tubal pregnancy, since the manipulated and damaged tube might not allow the fertilized egg to pass down. It should be emphasized that these are rare occurrences, but they can happen.

As with vasectomy, there are no long-term physical or health problems ordinarily associated with tubal ligation. The woman continues to ovulate and menstruate as usual, her hormone balance remains undisturbed, and her sexual responses are unchanged from any physical causes. However, a woman *can* become emotionally distressed later because of her inability to become pregnant, and this can be especially true when things happen that were never anticipated, or when circumstances suddenly change—a woman is divorced, for example, and later remarries and wishes desperately that she could have a baby by her new husband. Thus, *any* woman considering sterilization should make the decision only after careful, deliberate and, perhaps, lengthy consideration of any possible or foreseeable future fall of the cards.

For a young woman, for instance, with much of her childbearing life ahead of her, as well as an uncertain future, sterilization could be a very *bad* decision, considering the many excellent and reliable *reversible* birth control methods available. Unfortunately, considerations of convenience and emotional stress sometime lead to hasty, bad decisions when a little more time and consideration would have led a person away from them. A great many women have, for example, agreed to sterilization immediately after delivering a baby, being momentarily very tired of pregnancy and thinking how handy it would be to have the procedure done while they were already in the hospital anyway—or immediately after an abortion, often a time of much more emotional turmoil than usual. For many such women, these can in fact be the two *worst* times to make an irrevocable decision for a TL, but they are oftentimes when the woman is under great pressure from her doctor or family to decide—and *do* it—*right then*. And many women who have later bitterly regretted sterilization were those who made hurried or pressured decisions at such times.

It remains true that there are a great many women for whom sterilization can be a very *good* decision. For a woman in her late thirties or early forties, for example, who has already had all the children she ever wants to have by *anybody* under any circumstances, and who has a stable marriage or emotional relationship, a TL can simply relieve her of any further concern about pregnancy *ever*. For her a TL might be a mature and extremely sensible decision that she will never regret. It was for those whose decisions were perhaps not so mature or sensible that sterilization-reversal procedures were developed and—at least to a very limited degree so far—perfected.

STERILIZATION REVERSAL

Because there are, in fact, a great many young women or men who have had sterilization procedures done prematurely, and then bitterly regretted it later, what about *reversal* of sterilization? It is possible in some cases, and for either men or women, it might seem very simple—just take off the ligatures, open the tube ends, sew them back together again, and off we go.

In practice it isn't quite that simple—in fact, it can be very difficult. Reversing a vasectomy may be somewhat less of a problem than reversing a tubal ligation. For many men there is quite a bit of extra or redundant vas deferens. The surgeon can often remove the ties and the scar tissue back to the good tube on either end and suture the freshly cut ends together with microscopic sutures or stitches. Unfortunately, the procedure is lengthy and tedious. It requires a general anesthetic and involves microsurgical techniques —a means of magnifying the surgical field so that stitches as fine as cobweb can be used to join the cut ends of the tube together. The success of this procedure depends heavily on the individual skill and experience of the surgeon, and the very few surgeons in this country who have had enough skill and experience to boast a good track record (say, 50 percent successful reversals overall) may have their services booked up months in advance and may also command extremely high fees for their work, whether it is successful or not. And even when vasectomy reversal *is* successful, there is no guarantee that the man will be fertile. Some men develop immune reactions to their own sperm following vasectomy and may simply not produce potent sperm any more, reversal or no reversal.

The problem is even more difficult in reversing a tubal ligation. In most institutions, the first step is for the surgeon to perform a laparoscopy just to look at the tied and sectioned tubes to try to determine in advance if there is any reasonable hope, in the individual case, that either one of the tubes might be successfully rejoined. In many cases the answer may be no. If too much tube was removed or destroyed at the time of the TL, there may not be enough left to bring the two ends together again. This is often the case when the tube was obliterated by electrocautery and more tube was destroyed by the heat than was intended or expected. But even if the section of tube had been surgically excised, enough could have been taken and/or damaged by ligatures on either side, to make successful reconnection impossible. In other cases, the remnants of the tube may be so involved in scar tissue or so damaged by infection that reconnection cannot be accomplished.

If there is enough undamaged tube left to offer a possibility, the operation itself can then be done as an open abdominal procedure under general anesthesia, using microsurgical techniques. Even then there may be problems getting the cut ends of the tube perfectly matched and connected, since the tube is slightly funnel-shaped, with the upper end wider in diameter than the lower end.

Despite these problems, reversal *can* be accomplished successfully in some cases. Surgeons with wide experience, first in selecting good candidates for TL reversal, and then in performing the exacting surgery, have reported a high percentage of success, as much as 80 percent in some series. Such success records may be misleading, however, because only a small percentage of women who *want* sterilization reversal can qualify as "good candidates" for the procedure. And some health insurance plans may not cover the procedure, so it may be costly, too.

If you are a man or woman who wants to have a sterilization reversal operation considered, how can you go about it? Generally, the surgeons skilled in this operation are associated with a university hospital or some other major medical center or clinic. Any such medical center in your area should be able to refer you to the individual surgeons most skilled in reversal procedures. Certainly you will want to know any surgeon's ratio of successes in these operations, overall, and very possibly you may want a second surgeon's opinion before proceeding.

"REVERSIBLE STERILIZATION"

Considering the amount of interest in recent years in sterilization as a birth control method, and the problems involved in reversing these procedures as they are now performed, it's not surprising that doctors have been searching for some good way to perform "reversible sterilization"—*temporary* sterilization procedures that might provide some fairly simple means for reversal later with a much higher chance of success than is currently possible. So far no such "temporary" procedure has yet been perfected for general use, but several promising approaches are under investigation.

One method, for instance, involves the insertion of small silicone plugs into the lower ends of the Fallopian tubes where the tubes join the uterus. A D&C (dilatation and curettement) type operation, as described on page 138, has to be performed, and a sort of silicone "glue" is then squeezed up into the lower ends of the tubes. This "glue" then sets to form a solid plug on each side. The tubes themselves aren't manipulated or injured in any way—the plugs simply prevent sperm from going up the tube, or an ovum from coming down, as long as they are in place. And, in theory, the plugs can then later be removed simply by pulling them out in a similar D&C procedure. Theoretically, this should restore fertility in a high percentage of cases, since the intact tubes would be restored to use.

Another approach involves cutting the tubes but then, instead of tying them off and thus injuring tissue, simply enclosing the ends in small silicone bags secured to the outside of the tube with tiny sutures. The tubes can't grow together through the silicone, and when the bags are later removed, the tubes (in theory) could be reconnected surgically with greater success than if they had been severely injured, or had chunks cut out of them, during the TL. A similar approach could be used for vasectomy to offer better chances of later surgical reversal. A variation of this approach might be to enclose the whole upper end of the Fallopian tube in a silicone bag without cutting the tube at all. This would prevent the ovum from finding its way into the tube, and also prevent sperm from reaching the ovum until the bags were later removed.

None of these approaches, nor any others being considered, are yet perfected. When and if one of these methods, or some alternative, proves successful and reliable, this would then make sterilization on a temporary basis a far more plausible form of pregnancy protection for more women than permanent sterilization is today.

HYSTERECTOMY

One final—and quite irreversible—form of sterilization should be mentioned here, not because it is in any way a suitable method for birth control, but because it is an operation frequently performed for other medical reasons which —as an inevitable side effect—produces permanent and irreversible protection against pregnancy. This is a so-called hysterectomy, or surgical removal of the woman's uterus.

There are a number of medical reasons for such surgery—and in fact, it is very widely performed, especially among older women. The operation is commonly done, for example, to treat abnormally heavy uterine bleeding, or because of the formation of noncancerous but space-taking fibrous tumors called **fibroids** in the muscular wall of the uterus. When a hysterectomy is performed today, the uterus will be removed, often along with one or both tubes and ovaries if they are diseased and require removal. Some hysterectomies are performed by way of abdominal incisions, but in other cases the organ may be removed through the vagina in a so-called vaginal hysterectomy.

However it is done, a hysterectomy is a major surgical operation with very real risks attendant upon both the surgery itself and the general anesthesia that is required.

Since these risks are much greater than the risk attendant on tubal ligation alone, a hysterectomy is not ordinarily indicated solely as a means of sterilization—but sterilization is an obvious result when a hysterectomy is done for other reasons.

10

ABORTION

So far we have been outlining birth control methods—ways to avoid unwanted pregnancies, either by preventing conception in the first place or by preventing a fertilized ovum from becoming embedded in the uterus and developing into a pregnancy. This chapter is different, because abortion— the termination of a pregnancy that has already become established—is not truly a form of birth control at all. In fact, it represents a *failure* of birth control—a last-resort procedure to end a pregnancy that *hasn't* been prevented.

This is not the place to discuss the rights or wrongs of abortion, or to argue questions about the right of a fetus to life or the right of a woman to choose whether to carry a pregnancy or not. Right or wrong, abortion is a fact in the world today—it is one way that women the world over deal with the fact of unwanted pregnancy, and it is not going to go away soon no matter how any moral issues are resolved. For that reason, some factual information about abortion belongs in this book.

WHY ABORTION?

Medically speaking, the word *abortion* is a neutral term—it simply means the termination of a developing pregnancy, for whatever reason, whether from natural or unnatural causes. Doctors speak of a natural miscarriage or stillbirth as a *spontaneous abortion.* When medical conditions are such that a fetus has died naturally and is certain to be expelled, doctors will speak of *inevitable abortion.* When an abortion is deliberately precipitated at the wish of the mother, we speak of *induced* or *elective abortion,* and when this is done under circumstances that are against prevailing law, it is called *illegal abortion.*

Considering all the effective, reliable methods of birth control available in our society today, it is fair to ask why a woman should need an abortion in the first place. The most obvious reason is that there are still a great many women who don't want to become pregnant but don't use any birth control method regularly to prevent it because they just don't know how. This is especially true of young girls who are just beginning their sexual experience. It has been estimated that half of all the young people engaging in sex for the first time are taking *no precautions at all* against pregnancy. All too often these girls aren't *planning* to have sex at all but are simply carried away and trapped by their feelings. Often, at that point, they have no information about birth control, or are too embarrassed to discuss the matter with their partners if they do. It is here that advance knowledge about birth control can be so very important—a major reason for writing this book.

In addition, a certain number of undesired pregnancies occur even among people who *are* using birth control regularly. We have seen that there is no absolutely fail-safe birth control method short of hysterectomy. Even the very best birth control methods are only 99 or 99.5 percent effective—which means there is an occasional failure—and some methods are only 85 or 90 percent effective. And whereas many women can take a failure of birth control in stride and make peace with an accidental pregnancy, there are many others who will, for their own reasons, choose not to. For a few, a pregnancy that was acceptable at the time of conception becomes unacceptable later for one reason or another—a divorce, for example, or the death of a spouse. And finally, there are women who discover, through the sophisticated medical examinations now available, that they are carrying a fetus that is likely to have some grave or crippling disease or deformity and may choose to terminate the pregnancy even as late as three or four months along.

THE TIMING OF ABORTION

In modern countries with high-quality medical facilities it is possible to induce abortion with a high degree of safety to the woman all the way up to the twenty-eighth week of pregnancy—the end of the sixth month. However, with a pregnancy that far advanced, a baby could survive. Thus, for practical and ethical considerations, it is extremely uncommon in this country to perform an abortion after the twentieth week of pregnancy—the end of the fifth month.

Having said that, there is also a blanket medical consideration: when an abortion is to be done, the earlier it is done, the better. Obstetricians divide a nine-month pregnancy into three, three-month segments, or "trimesters." An abortion performed during the first twelve weeks of pregnancy—the first three months, or trimester—is by far the easiest to perform and the easiest on the woman, with the least possible hospital time, cost, and morbidity—the medical term for illness or complications. After twelve weeks more complicated abortion techniques must be used, and the woman is likely to have more "down time," more expense, and greater risk of complications.

Historically, abortions have been performed for centuries by a wide variety of methods. Various instruments would be introduced into the uterus through the cervix, or toxic products and other **abortifacients** (abortion-producing agents) taken by mouth or packed into the vagina or cervix to induce abortion. Many of these "home remedy" abortions were highly dangerous to the woman as well as the fetus, and such complications as life-threatening hemorrhage or massive infection were common. As little as twenty years ago in this country, when abortion was almost universally illegal, abortions were done hastily, furtively, and carelessly, under filthy conditions, often with unsterilized instruments, and death of the woman from **septicemia** (blood poisoning) was commonplace. Legalization of abortion has put an end to this horror story. Today abortions are performed by skilled and careful practitioners, in clean medical surroundings, without haste or threat, and with sterile instruments and careful follow-up to protect the woman against postoperative complications and deal with them quickly and effectively whenever they occur.

ABORTION BEFORE
TWELVE WEEKS

Abortion during the early weeks (the first trimester) of a pregnancy may be performed either by **dilatation and curettement (D&C)** or by **vacuum aspiration** of the uterus. Both procedures are generally performed under local anesthetic, though in unusual circumstances a brief general anesthesia may be used. With the D&C, the cervical canal is dilated with a series of metal tubes and the uterine lining is then scraped, or *curetted*, to dislodge the implanted fetus. The procedure is very safe, takes about five to ten minutes, and then is all over. In most cases the woman can go home the same day or the following morning at the latest.

There is one major problem with the D&C method: even very early in pregnancy, blood vessels in the uterus will have begun to enlarge to support the pregnancy, and the part of the uterine wall where the pregnancy is lodged will be softer than usual. Thus the D&C method is sometimes accompanied by a significant amount of bleeding, or —very rarely—the curetting instrument may penetrate the uterus. Because of such possible complications, the vacuum aspiration method is often preferred. Again the cervical canal must be dilated, and a metal or plastic tube inserted into the uterus. This tube is then connected to a suction pump, and the pregnancy is sucked out. In most cases, after the patient wakes up, there is no more bleeding than during a normal period, and, again, she can go home within a few hours. As to the risk to the mother with either of these methods, it is significantly lower than the risk involved in carrying a pregnancy to term.

ABORTION AFTER
TWELVE WEEKS

After the first three months of pregnancy, however, the fetus has become large enough that dilating the cervix and either curetting or suctioning the uterine lining becomes more risky, so other abortion methods are preferred. One technique sometimes used is called **dilatation and evacuation (D&E).** The cervix is again dilated after general anesthesia, but the larger fetus must then be crushed and evacuated from the uterus in pieces. Like the D&C or vacuum aspiration method, it has the advantage of being all over with when the patient awakens, but the risk of postoperative bleeding or of incomplete removal of the fetus is greater, and it becomes an unpleasant operation for the medical and nursing staff.

Alternative methods involve the use of some kind of medicine which will start the uterus contracting, causing the woman to miscarry the baby. Irritating solutions may be injected into the uterus through the abdominal wall, or through the cervical canal. In addition, drugs known as **prostaglandins** may be used—hormone-like substances that cause the uterine muscle to contract.

— 139 —

These techniques are safe when performed for later pregnancies, but they are not *immediate,* as are the direct methods discussed above. The woman may have to wait several hours for the uterus to start contracting, and perhaps hours longer for the miscarriage to occur. Bleeding is not ordinarily a problem, but occasionally the placenta or after-birth may not be expelled with the fetus, so that a D&C may have to be performed later to remove it. Thus, while the method is safe enough in the long run, it may be far more traumatic and uncomfortable for the woman.

In extreme or special cases other techniques may be used. In some cases, when the pregnancy to be terminated has advanced to the fifth or sixth month (the end of the second trimester) before the decision is made, abortion may require a **hysterectomy**—a major abdominal operation under general anesthesia, essentially a "mini-Caesarian," in which the uterus is opened and the fetus removed. And in cases in which an older woman has already had all the children she intends to have, an abortion may be performed via hysterectomy—total removal of uterus, fetus and all—thus solving any question of future pregnancies.

CONSEQUENCES OF ABORTION

In the past a great deal has been written about the possible consequences of abortion on a woman's emotional health and her future ability to have children. When abortions are done today by skilled surgeons in clean, modern medical facilities under circumstances of legality, the chances of any bad physical consequences are very remote. It is estimated that fewer than 1 percent of all women who have abortions have any physical problems at all at the time of abortion, and far fewer suffer any long-term physical disabilities. Properly done, an abortion should have no effect on a woman's future fertility, nor cause any future problem with childbearing.

The possible emotional consequences of an abortion

cannot be defined so clearly, simply because they depend so much on how an individual woman feels about having ended a pregnancy in this way. There are women who later bitterly regret having had an abortion and wish they had carried the baby and either kept it or offered it for adoption. There are others who have continuing, perhaps very disturbing, guilt feelings about having had an abortion, or who allow others to make them feel guilty—and there are surely those in our society who are eager to assign guilt to any woman who has an abortion. About all that can be said about these possibilities is that the time to consider possible emotional consequences very carefully is *before* deciding on an abortion, since this is obviously not a decision that can be retracted once it has been made and acted upon. Certainly *any* woman contemplating an abortion should carefully consider and explore all alternatives available; and any woman who finds herself in doubt or concerned about later emotional consequences should also seek counseling—from physicians, social or psychological counselors, religious counselors, close friends, or whomever one can trust the most before making a decision.

At the time of this writing, abortion on demand is legally available to any woman anywhere in the United States, supported by a 1973 landmark decision of the United States Supreme Court. Just how long this legal position will prevail, no one can say. The question of abortion on demand, or the legal or moral propriety of abortion at all, is now a matter of vigorous and sometimes violent national debate, and even the Supreme Court can modify or reverse its own decisions. But even under current circumstances, abortion is at best a poor second to rational, responsible birth control methods, and should at best remain what it is —a court of last resort when all else has failed.

BIRTH CONTROL
IN THE FUTURE

In chapter two we described an "ideal birth control method"—a method, we hastened to point out, which does not exist. Until that ideal has been reached, the search for new or better contraceptives will continue. Although many birth control methods we have already discussed have been in use for decades, some are fairly recent innovations. The low-dosage combination pill, for example, has been fully developed only in the last ten years in hope of correcting some of the disadvantages of higher-dose estrogen/progesterone oral contraceptives. And the vaginal sponge barrier method discussed in chapter five was introduced for general use only in 1984.

Some methods have probably been perfected about as much as possible—any modifications or improvements are likely to be fairly minor. Nobody, for example, foresees any great breakthroughs in natural, or "rhythm method," contraception. Recently a manufacturer introduced a rather expensive electronic thermometer combined with a computerized memory and calculating device which might provide slightly greater accuracy in measuring basal body temperatures and managing calendar calculations to help identify ovulation time, but this is just a refinement of the basic methods we discussed, not any great step forward. The future may well see the discovery and introduction of more effective, more rapid-acting spermicides for use with barrier type contraceptives, but these will add very little to overall effectiveness of barrier methods, and the barrier devices thmselves are unlikely to be improved greatly except in minor matters of fit or aesthetics. Now research with IUDs is largely concerned with exploring questions of safety rather than of effectiveness. And the testing of abortion-inducing drugs such as RU 486 doesn't solve the problem of better ways to prevent conception in the first place.

But if few major improvements can be expected in existing birth control methods, a few completely new approaches to contraception are under investigation today and may well play a part in effective, reliable birth control in the future.

A "PILL" FOR MEN

Men have as important a role in prevention of unwanted pregnancies as women do—but only a few birth control methods deal in any way with controlling *male* fertility. The condom is *used* by the male partner but of course has no effect on his production of sperm cells. Vasectomy is the only really effective method of controlling male fertility today, and although it has proven popular and acceptable to many men, it carries the great disadvantage that it is likely to be irreversible in most cases. But if there are "pills" for women, why not "pills" for men?

Several drugs have been studied that might fulfill the role—drugs that can temporarily reduce or stop the production of sperm cells but would allow recovery of sperm-generating ability when the medicine was stopped. Most that have been studied have presented serious problems. Any drug that reduces sperm production requires a long while—perhaps weeks or even months—to be effective, with live, viable sperm still present and available for a long while after the medicine is started. Once discontinued, the effects of these drugs take an equal or longer time to wear off. Therefore this may never be a *fast* approach to contraception, nor quickly reversible. Another problem also exists —drugs that reduce or block sperm production also tend to reduce the man's sexual interest, or even his ability to perform sexually at all—not exactly the effect one would seek out in a birth control method. And some drugs also have other side effects.

Perhaps the most promising male pill, currently under investigation in China, contains a derivative of cottonseed oil known as **gossypol.** This drug seems to impair the ability of sperm to fertilize ova, but leads to such side effects as muscular weakness and depletion of potassium, one of the vital electrolytes, in the user's body. Some studies suggest that very low doses of this drug may be effective for birth control yet avoid most of the side effects—but results of these studies may not be in for another ten or fifteen years. In other places, such as Latin America, various other plant extracts are being studied as possible male contraceptives, but it is too early to know results. Finally, some laboratories are exploring "sperm maturation inhibitors" that might interfere with the fertilizing capabilities of sperm.

MORE REVERSIBLE
STERILIZATION

In chapter ten we mentioned some experimental methods being studied to make tubal ligations in women more readily reversible. Surgeons have also been studying techniques that might make vasectomy in the male more readily reversible. One idea is to install a small two-way valve or tap in the vas deferens. When the valve is closed, movement of sperm up the vas is blocked; when it is reopened (theoretically a very simple, perhaps even self-administered procedure) the sperm can move freely again and fertility can be restored. All this, of course, is still theoretical at present. Such valves have been tested, but it is far too early to assess their effectiveness.

NEW HORMONE
INNOVATIONS

The hormone contraceptives women use today are all based upon various combinations of the female sex hormones estrogen and progesterone, or on progesterone alone. The production of estrogen, as we have seen, is triggered by production of follicle-stimulating hormone, or FSH, by the pituitary gland. Recently, however, researchers have been studying another "control hormone" known as **gonadotrophin releasing hormone,** or **GnRH,** which is produced in the **hypothalamus,** a part of the brain directly connected to the pituitary gland. Production of FSH in the pituitary can be speeded up or slowed down by small pulses of GnRH; if the pituitary is subjected to an overload of this hormone, it simply temporarily shuts down production of FSH and luteinizing hormone, or LH, as well, thus bringing ovulation to a temporary halt.

GnRH has been tested as a possible substitute birth control hormone. There are some problems. As a protein, it is digested in the stomach when taken by mouth, so injection has been necessary. As an alternative to injections, however, studies have shown that it can be administered as a nasal spray, with enough hormone for effective contraception being absorbed through the mucous membranes in the nose. So far woman who have tested this method in such countries as Scotland and Sweden have found it satisfactory, with no ill effects—but the GnRH hormone today is extremely expensive. This method may become more widely available and practical when it has been more extensively tested for safety and when production methods allow the hormone to be sold inexpensively.

SKIN PATCH
CONTRACEPTIVES

Swallowing pills every day is a drag for some women. How much better if pill-type hormones could be enclosed in a skin patch that would allow hormones to be absorbed through the skin for 12, 24, 36, or 48 hours after application! Better or not, this is another route of administration that is being explored for birth control hormones.

ANTI-PREGNANCY
VACCINES

This is perhaps the farthest reach as a possible contraceptive method, and the farthest in the future of all investigatory methods, but it is being studied. In theory, vaccines could be made against sperm cells for use by either men or women, or against the outer layer of the ovum, for use by women, or against pregnancy itself—for example, a vaccine against the hormone known as **human chorionic gonadotrophin,** or **HCG,** which is produced in the woman almost as soon as fertilization takes place and is essential for the maintenance of the pregnancy. (Detecting the early appearance of HCG in the woman's bloodstream and urine immediately after conception is the basis for nearly all modern pregnancy tests). The first two kinds of vaccines might provide good temporary contraception without interfering in any way with hormones or ovulation, but present so many scientific and laboratory problems that years of study of such vaccines in experimental animals will be necessary before any testing in humans can be attempted. Any vaccine against a human pregnancy hormone not only involves problems of safety and reversibility, but ethical problems as well, and even if found scientifically possible, may never prove to be an acceptable birth control method for humans.

Whatever the future may hold, many safe, effective and acceptable birth control methods already exist, as we have explored in this book—enough different methods to meet the needs of virtually any woman who wishes to avoid unwanted pregnancies, or any couple who wish to have control over the size and timing of their families. Some methods are best suited to some peoples' needs, other methods to others'—but it is hard to imagine any situation or circumstance that cannot be met satisfactorily by one method or another.

No one method is absolutely ideal or failure-free, but time and again experience has proven that *any* method is all the more failure-free the more intelligently, carefully, and diligently it is applied. Obviously, no birth control method will work unless it is used. You cannot use a birth control method unless you know about it, understand how it works, and are willing to apply it. This book provides the knowledge you need to pick a birth control method suitable to *your* needs and to apply it effectively—and thus to exercise reasonable, intelligent control over a very important aspect of your life. Put it to good use.

GLOSSARY

Note: Specific organs of the male and female body are not included in this glossary. Definitions and illustrations of them may be found by referring to the index.)

Abdominal laparotomy—an exploratory operation of the abdomen.

Abortifacient—a drug or chemical that can cause an abortion or the loss of a pregnancy.

Androgens—the male sex hormones produced mainly in the testicles and the cortex of the adrenal glands.

Bi-phasic pill—a kind of birth control pill containing two different amounts of hormones for different times of the month.

Celibacy—not having sex at all with another person.

Chromosomes—clusters of hereditary material (DNA) in the nucleus of living cells.

Coitus interruptus—withdrawal of the man's penis before ejaculation of sperm while having sex.

Conception—the joining together of a sperm cell and a ripened egg cell, or ovum, to form a fertilized ovum—the beginning of a pregnancy.

Condom—a rubber sheath that can be rolled down over the penis before sex to keep sperm out of the vagina and protect against infection.

Contraceptive—any drug, device or sex technique used to prevent conception.

Corpus luteum—the nest of cells in an ovary from which a ripened ovum was released.

Deoxyribonucleic acid (DNA)—the large spiral-shaped molecules that make up each cell's hereditary material. DNA molecules link together to form *genes*, which line up to form chromosomes in the cell's nucleus.

Diaphragm—a dome-shaped rubber device which fits into the vagina and covers the cervix to prevent sperm from entering the uterus during sex (See Fig. 00, p. 00).

Dilatation and curettement (D&C)—an operation to dilate the opening in the cervix and scrape out the inside of the uterus. Sometimes used to perform an abortion during the first twelve weeks of pregnancy.

Dilatation and evacuation (D&E)—an operation to dilate the opening in the cervix and suck out or evacuate a fetus. Often used to perform an abortion.

Douching—rinsing out the vagina with water, diluted vinegar solution or other solutions.

Ectopic—"in the wrong place." An ectopic pregnancy is a dangerous, abnormal condition in which a pregnancy develops in a tube instead of inside the uterus.

Ejaculation—release of sperm during a male sexual climax.

Elective abortion—an abortion (removal of a pregnancy) performed at the wish or choice of the woman.

Electrocautery—a surgical instrument equipped with an electrically heated wire, used for cutting or burning (cauterizing) tissue or controlling bleeding.

Embryo—a pregnancy in the earliest stage of development, from the time of conception to the end of the eighth week in the uterus.

Erection—enlargement and stiffening of the man's penis due to sexual excitement. The same thing occurs, to a lesser degree, to the woman's clitoris during sexual stimulation.

Estrogens—female sex hormones produced mainly in the ovaries.

Fibroids—benign (non-cancerous) growths of fibrous tissue that sometimes form in the muscular wall of the uterus.

Follicle—a nest of cells in the ovary containing the "bud" of a future egg cell or ovum.

Follicle-stimulating hormone (FSH)—a hormone, released by the pituitary gland, which can trigger the ripening of an egg cell in its follicle in the ovary.

Gametes (germ cells)—special sex cells that contain only half the hereditary material as other cells in the body. The sperm cell is the male gamete. The egg cell or ovum is the female gamete.

Genes—clusters of DNA molecules that form the basic units of hereditary material in each cell. Genes are passed from parent to child and determine such characteristics of the child as its sex, skin color, hair or eye color, etc.

Genitals—the male or female sex or reproductive organs.

Gonadotrophin releasing hormone (GnRH)—a hormone manufactured by the brain which triggers production of follicle-stimulating hormone by the pituitary gland. Important in starting off a new ovulation cycle in the woman.

Gossypol—a chemical which interferes with sperm function. One of the experimental "male contraceptives" under investigation.

Hematoma—a collection of blood that has leaked into the tissue outside a blood vessel and then clotted.

Hormones—powerful chemicals formed in certain glands and organs of the body and carried by the bloodstream to affect the behavior of other organs.

Human chorionic gonadotrophin (HCG)—a hormone produced in the uterus almost immediately after a new pregnancy has started to grow. Detecting this hormone in the bloodstream is an important early test for pregnancy.

Hypothalamus—a hormone-producing portion of the brain close to the pituitary gland.

Hysterectomy—surgical removal of the uterus.

Hysterotomy—a surgical opening into the uterus performed, for example, when a baby is to be delivered by Caesarian section.

Interstitial cell stimulating hormone—a male hormone that triggers the production of sperm cells in the testicles.

Intrauterine contraceptive device (IUD)—a small plastic device placed inside the uterus to prevent pregnancies. Once inserted it can be left in place for months or years to act as a contraceptive.

Laparoscopy—a surgical procedure in which a narrow, lighted tube or *laparoscope* is inserted into the abdomen through a tiny incision so that the surgeon can inspect the ovaries, tubes and uterus by direct vision. **Culdoscopy** is a similar procedure in which the scope is inserted up into the lower abdomen through the vaginal wall.

Luteinizing hormone (LH)—a hormone produced after ovulation to help prepare the inner lining of the uterus for a pregnancy.

Meiosis—the process by which the male or female sex cells or *gametes* are formed, with each cell containing only half the hereditary material of a normal cell.

Menopause—the time of life, usually around age fifty, when a woman no longer produces reproductive cells and ceases to have menstrual periods.

Mini-pill—a kind of birth control pill that contains only the hormone *progesterone* without any estrogen.

Mitosis—the normal, usual form of cell division in which each daughter cell receives 100% of the hereditary material from the parent cell.

Mittelschmerz—a German word meaning "pain in the middle." A brief, cramping pain some women feel in the abdomen at the time a ripened ovum is released from an ovary.

Motile—able to move around from place to place.

Nocturnal emission—an involuntary release of sperm cells, usually at night, as a result of a sexually exciting dream.

Nonoxynol-9—a sperm-killing chemical, the active ingredient in most *spermicidal* (sperm-killing) gels or vaginal foams.

Oral contraceptive pills (OCs)—pills containing hormones, taken by the woman to prevent ovulation and thus prevent pregnancy. Popularly known as "the Pill."

Orgasm—the sexual climax in male or female—the peak of sexual pleasure during sex. Accompanied by ejaculation, or release of sperm in the male.

Ovaries—the sex glands in the female where the egg cell (ovum) is formed and released.

Ovulation—the release of a ripened egg cell, or ovum, from the ovary where it was formed. Upon release it travels down the Fallopian tube toward the uterus.

Ovum (pl. **Ova)**—a female reproductive cell, the egg cell.

Pelvic inflammatory disease (PID)—a chronic infection in the tubes, often due to gonorrhea or other sexually transmitted infections. Infection in this area can damage and block the tubes, making the woman infertile or unable to conceive.

Pituitary gland—a vital hormone-producing gland connected to the underside of the brain.

Placenta—a special organ that develops inside the uterus during pregnancy to provide nutrients and oxygen to the growing fetus and which is expelled after giving birth.

Progesterone—a female sex hormone that helps support the ovum until it is fertilized and protects the growth of the new baby if pregnancy occurs.

Progestogen—one of a number of hormones, some laboratory-made, which mimic or copy the action of progesterone.

Prolactin—a hormone that works with estrogens to enlarge a pregnant woman's breasts and enable them to produce milk. Also called *lactogenic hormone*.

Prophylaxis—prevention of infection or disease. Condoms, which protect against sexually transmitted diseases, are sometimes called *"prophylactics."*

Prostaglandins—hormones produced in the uterus and other organs which (among other things) sometimes produce menstrual cramping or other muscle spasm.

Prostate gland—a male located gland just below the bladder which produces the *seminal fluid* that carries the sperm out during ejaculation.

Puberty—the time of sexual maturation; that is, the time when both males and females become physically able to reproduce.

Reproductive system—the sex organs in males and females which make it possible for couples to have children.

Rhythm method—a method of birth control which involves avoiding sex during the time each month when the woman is fertile (i.e., several days before, during, and after the time when she ovulates).

Secondary sex characteristics—those bodily manifestations of sexual maturity that are not directly related to reproduction but which essentially prepare the body for it. For example, the appearance of pubic hair, breast development in the girl, enlargement of the sex organs, etc.

Septicemia—blood poisoning; a dangerous kind of infection in which bacteria have entered the blood stream.

Sperm granuloma—a cyst containing sperm which sometimes forms in the scrotum just below the place where a man's tubes have been tied.

Spermicide—a chemical which kills sperm on contact.

Sterilization—an operation to make a man or woman sterile (unable to reproduce). A tubal ligation (TL) in the woman, or a vasectomy in the man.

The Pill—a common nickname for oral contraceptive pills (OCs) which contain hormones to be taken by the woman to prevent ovulation.

Thrombus—a blood clot that forms in a blood vessel. A rare complication in some women taking the Pill.

Toxic shock syndrome (TSS)—a group of symptoms, including fever, skin rash, and collapse, caused by poisons produced by certain staph bacteria growing in the vagina or elsewhere and recently found to be related to the use of "super absorbent" tampons.

Tri-phasic pill—a kind of birth control pill containing three different amounts of hormones for different times of the month.

Tubal ligation (TL)—an operation in which a woman's Fallopian tubes are tied and cut on both sides to cause sterilization.

Vacuum aspiration—a method of abortion in which the fetus is drawn out of the uterus with a suction instrument.

Vasectomy—an operation in which the vas deferens in the male is cut and tied on both sides to cause sterilization.

INDEX

Abdominal laparotomy, 126, 149
Abortifacient, 138, 149
Abortion, 43–45, 135
    after twelve weeks, 139–40
    before twelve weeks,
      138–39
    consequences of, 140–41
    elective, 43
    illegal, 136
    timing of, 137–38
Acne, 31
Advantages, 47–48
    condom, 72, 74
    IUD, 115
    mini-pill, 103–04
AIDS, 40
Ampicillin, 92
Androgens, 23, 25, 28, 31, 149

Barrier methods, 40–43, 67
    chemical, 68–69, 71
    condom, 44, 71–72, 74–76
    diaphragm, 44, 76, 78–81

    spermicidal, 44, 68–69, 71
    sterilization, 42
    vaginal sponge, 44, 81–82
Barrier of time and space.
    See Rhythm method
Basal body temperature, 59–61
Beard, 25
Birth control, 143–46
    anti-pregnancy vaccines,
      147–48
    definition of, 14–17
    menu, 44–45
    permanent, 42–43
    reversible, 42
Bi-phasic pills, 88, 149
Bleeding, 86, 88, 94
    uterine, 132
Blood clots, 86–87, 95–96
Blood poisoning. *See* Septicemia
Breakthrough bleeding.
    See Bleeding
Breast tenderness, 88
Buds, 28

Calendar
    for ovulation, 54
Cancer, 93–96
Celibacy, 15, 39–40, 149
Centers for Disease Control, 95
Cervical mucus, 61
Cervix, 27, 33
Chemical barriers.
    See Spermicidal barriers
Chemical messengers, 23
Chromosomes, 149
Coitus interruptus, 71, 149
Combination pills, 88
Conception, 15, 149
Condoms, 16, 67, 71, 75–76,
    149, 152
    advantages of, 72, 74
    disadvantages of, 74
    failure, 47
    with the Pill, 91
    venereal diseases, 16
Constant fertility, 27
Contraceptive, 150
Corpus luteum, 32–33, 150
Cramping, 115, 153
Culdoscopy, 126, 151
Cycles, 56

D&C, 131, 138, 140, 150
D&E 139, 150
Daughter cells, 20
Deoxyribonuleic acid. *See* DNA
Depo-Provera, 107
Diabetes, 96
Diaphragm, 67, 150
    failure, 47
    Pill, 91
Dilatation and curettement.
    See D&C
Dilation and evacuation.
    See D&E
Disadvantages
    condom, 74
    IUD, 115–17

mini-pill, 104–07
natural birth control, 48
spermicidal barriers, 69
DNA, 20, 150
Douching, 13, 16, 150

Ectopic, 105, 150
Effectiveness
    IUD, 111
    Pill, 46, 97
Egg cell. *See* Ovum
Egypt, 16
Ejaculation, 15, 150, 152
Elective abortion, 43–44, 136
Electrocautery, 124, 130, 150
Embryo, 35, 150
Erection, 23, 150
Estrogens, 28, 32, 150
    secondary sex
        characteristics, 31
Estrus makers, 28

Failure
    condom, 47
    diaphragm, 47
    spermicidal barriers, 47
    See also Abortion
Fallopian tubes, 26–28, 32
    See also TL
Female reproductive cycle,
    27–28
    menstruation, 34–37
    ovulation, 31–34
Female sex hormones.
    See Estrogens
Female sterilization.
    See TL
Fertile period, 57, 59–61
Fertility awareness.
    See Rhythm method
Fertilization, 15, 26, 35, 39
Fertilized ovum, 53
    prevent implantation, 41–42
Fibroids, 132, 150

Follicles, 28, 31, 150
Follicle-stimulating hormone.
  See FSH
Food and Drug Administration,
  106, 112
FSH, 31, 150

Gametes, 19–20, 22, 151, 152
Genes, 20, 151
Genital herpes, 40
Genitals, 23, 151
Genetic material, 20
Germ cells, 19
  See also Gametes
GnRH, 151
Gold standard, 45–47
Gonadotrophin releasing
  hormone. See GnRH
Gonorrhea, 93

Half cells, 19–20, 32
  special destiny, 22
HCG, 147, 151
Heart, 95–96
Heat, 28
Hematoma, 121, 151
Heredity, 20
High blood pressure, 96
Homosexual, 40
Hormone contraceptives, 99,
  107–08
  mini-pill, 100–06
  morning-after, 109
Hormone medicines, 45
  prevent ovulation, 16
Hormones, 23, 151
  pregnancy-protecting, 33
Human chorionic gonadotrophin
  See HCG
Hypothalamus, 151
Hysterectomy, 15, 132–33, 140,
  151
Hysterotomy, 151

ICSH, 25, 151
Ideal contraceptive, 17–18
Immune system, 123, 129
Implantation, preventing, 41–42
Interstitial cell stimulating
  hormone. See ICSH
Interstitial cells, 23
Intrauterine contraceptive
  Device. See IUDs
IUDs, 42, 45, 109, 111–12,
  116–17, 151
  advantages of, 115
  disadvantages of, 115–17
  effectiveness, 111
  how it works, 113

Journal of the American
  Medical Association, 90

Kidney disease, 96

Lactogenic hormone, 33, 153
Laparoscope, 151
Laparoscopy, 126, 151
LH, 32, 151
Liver disease, 96
Luteinizing hormone.
  See LH

Male reproductive system, 23,
  25–27
Male sex hormone.
  See Androgen
Male sterilization.
  See Vasectomy
Marker, Russell, 84
Masturbation, 26
Meiosis, 20, 152
Menfegol, 68
Menopause, 35, 152
Menstrual cycle, 15–16,
  See also Menstruation
Menstruation, 34–37
Mexican yams, 84

Middle Ages, 16
Milk-producing hormone, 33
Mini-Caesarian, 140
Mini-pill, 88, 100–06, 152
   advantages of, 103–04
   disadvantages of, 104–05
   how it is used, 101–03
Mitosis, 20, 152
Mittelschmerz, 34, 60, 152
Morning-after contraception,
   109
Mumps, 27

Natural birth control, 15, 40–41,
   49, 65
   celibacy, 44
   coitus interruptus, 44,
     50–52
   disadvantages, 48
   homosexuality, 44
   nursing, 44, 64–65
   rhythm method, 44, 52–54,
     56–57, 59–64
   withdrawal, 50–52
Nocturnal emission, 26, 152
Nonoxynol-9, 68, 152
Normal cells, 19–20
Nursing, 64–65

OC's 41, 152
One-cycle packets, 89
Oral contraceptives. See OC's
Orgasm, 26, 152
Outside the body, 15
Ova. See Ovum
Ovaries, 28, 31, 152
   See also Ovum
Ovulation, 31–34, 40, 152
   cycle, 35
   preventing, 41
Ovulation, pinpointing
   cervical mucus, 61
   charting basal body
     temperature, 59–61

   charting cycles, 56–57
   estimate fertile period, 57,
     59
   keeping a calendar, 54, 56
Ovum, 15, 28, 152
   fertilized, 19
   hormone medicine, 16

Pain in the middle, 34, 152
   See also Mittelschmerz
Pap smears, 94
Parent cell, 20
Pelvic inflammatory disease.
   See PID
Pelvis, 23, 27
Penil sheath, 71–72, 74–76
Penis, 23, 25
Periodic abstinence.
   See Rhythm method
Phasic pills, 88
PID, 116, 152
Pill, 41, 83, 90
   advantages, 92–94
   age, 13
   ampicillin, 92
   basic pill, 44
   bi-phasic, 44
   blood clotting, 95–96
   cancer, 93–96
   diabetes, 96
   disadvantages of, 48, 94–
     97
   discovery of, 84–85
   drug interactions, 91–92
   early pill, 85–88
   early problems, 85–88
   effectiveness of, 46, 97
   health benefits, 93
   heart disease, 96
   high blood pressure, 96
   kidney disease, 96
   liver disease, 96
   modern pill, 88–89
   Rifampin, 92

Pill (*continued*)
    side effects, 94–97
    smoking, 95–96
    strokes, 95–96
    Tetracycline, 92
    tri-phasic, 44
    using, 89–92
    who should not use it,
      95–96
Pimples, 31
Pituitary gland, 25, 31, 33, 152
Placenta, 35, 152
Planned Parenthood, 63
Pod, 28
Pregnancy, 12–15, 19–20,
    22–23, 25–28, 31–37
Progesterone, 33, 35, 84, 88,
    108–09, 152
Progesterone-only pill.
    See Mini-pill
Progestogen, 84, 107–08, 153
Prolactin, 33, 64, 153
Prophylactics, 153
Prophylaxis, 153
Prostaglandins, 139, 153
Prostrate gland, 23, 153
Puberty, 28, 153
Pubic hair, 25, 28

Religious convictions, 16
Rifampin, 92
Reproductive system, 22, 153
Rhythm method, 40, 52–53, 58,
    62–64, 153
    advantages of, 61–62
    disadvantages of, 62–64
    fertility cycle, 16
    ovulation, 54, 56–57, 59–61

Scrotum, 23
Secondary sex characteristics,
    25, 28, 153
    estrogens, 31
Second hormone, 32

Seminal fluid, 153
Seminal vesicles, 23
Septicemia pills, 138, 153
Sequential pills, 88
Sex cells, 19–20
Sex glands, 28
Sex hormones.
    See Androgens, Estrogens
Sexual climax, 26
Sexual maturity, 23
Sheath. *See* Condoms
Shell, 28
Smoking, 95–96
Sperm cells, 15, 19, 23, 28
    life of, 25–27
Sperm granuloma, 121, 153
    life of, 25–27
Spermicidal barriers, 70
    advantages of, 69
    aerosols, 69, 71
    condom, 71–76
    creams, 69
    disadvantages of, 67
    failure, 47
    foams, 46–47
    jellies, 69
    vaginal inserts, 68–69
    vaginal suppositories, 68–69
Spermicide, 68, 152
Sponge, 44, 67, 81–82
Spontaneous abortion, 136
Spotting, 89–90
Sterile, 27
Sterilization, 18, 119–20,
    126–27, 153
    female, 124, 126–28
    hysterectomy, 43, 45,
      132–33
    irreversible, 43
    male, 120–21, 123–24
    reversal, 128–32
    tubal ligation, 45, 124,
      126–28
    See also Vasectomy

Stillbirth.
  See Spontaneous abortion
Strokes, 95–96
Syntex Corporation, 85
Synthetic progestogens, 84–85

Testes, 23
Testicles, 23, 25, 28
Tetracycline. *See* Pill
Thromboses, 86–87
Thrombus, 153
TL, 42, 124, 126–28, 153, 154
Toxic shock syndrone. *See* TSS
Tri-phasic pills, 88, 154
  See also Pill
TSS, 153–54
Tubal Ligation. *See* TL

Urethra, 23
Urinary bladder, 23
Uterine cancer, 107
Uterus, 27
  bleeding, 132
  hysterectomy, 15
U.S. Food and Drug
  Administration, 85

Vacuum aspiration, 138, 154
Vagina, 27
Vaginal film, 67
Vaginal hysterectomy, 132
Vaginal sponge, 67
  See also Barrier methods
Vas deferens, 23, 123
  reversal, 129
Vasectomy, 42, 45, 120–21,
  123–24, 153–54
  emotional effects of, 123
  hematoma, 121
  immune reactions, 123
  problems, 121
Vatican Roulette, 62
Venereal disease, 16
Voice box, 25
Vulva, 27

Wet dream, 26
Withdrawal, 50–52
World Health Organization,
  88–89

Yellow body, 32